CZEC

PAST

To: Debbie,

Best Wishes,

Beverly A Hajek

STÁTNÍ ZNAKY REPUBLIKY ČESKOSLOVENSKÉ
ARMOIRIES DE LA RÉPUBLIQUE TCHÉCOSLOVAQUE

PRAVDA VÍTĚZÍ

INTRODUCTION

CZECHered PAST is a true story about an amazing man born in 1890, the fate that changed his life and how he overcame heartbreaking obstacles. This story was kept in a secret place deep in his heart and mind, never sharing one word with his family for 50 years. Not until seconds before his death in 1963 did he realize the importance of enlightening his heirs, but of course it was too late at that point. Almost 30 years after his death, his son stumbled upon a revelation that sent shock waves through the entire family. Now it was up to someone to do extensive research and try to piece the puzzle together.

The author cunningly weaves the facts into an intriguing story filled with history, memories and triumphant events that transformed this mans' prolific life. The story finds its way from Czechoslovakia (Czech Republic) to Texas and finally to several eastern states. Not until 2015 did the author feel prepared to tackle this larger-than-life story and introduce it to the world.

CZECHered PAST

4

7

12

15

16

23

A 100 year old family secret uncovered.

BEVERLY A. HAJEK

CZECHered PAST:

Library of Congress Control Number: 2016914409
Beverly A. Hajek, Waynesboro, PA

ISBN: 978-0-9979294-0-9

Published by BB Publishers

www.BBPublishers.com

ACKNOWLEDGEMENTS:

The adage that "it takes a village" has certainly applied to this project. It is with sincere, heartfelt gratitude that I wish to thank those friends and family members who supported me along this journey. As a debut novelist, I found it reassuring to know that these folks were both my safety net and my cheerleading squad.

A special thanks to our Texas cousins who most graciously shared photos and memories of the portion of Edwards' life that we were sadly unaware of details. Julie Taylor, Norma Lee Daniel, Helen McDonald and Sharon Matzner provided a fountain of information that helped piece this puzzle together. The late Edward W. Hajek and his wife, Nina, were a treasure trove of stories and facts that were woven into this true story.

An invaluable piece of this story was obtained from my husband, Richard J. Hajek (who is a walking dictionary) and his sister, Dr. Jacqueline Werner who patiently shared documents, photos and memories of their life growing up with their Father, Edward.

Special recognition should go to my readers who so graciously and persistently read and re-read early drafts. They helped me to realize that sometimes you can get so close to a storyline that you assume the public is viewing an event the same way you are. My team of readers was: Jan Wagaman, Janet Mowery, William Freienmuth, Patricia Donnelly, Mary Glessner, Karen Day and Beverly Robinson, who also assisted with computer layout.

I will always be thankful for such a strong network. God surely does provide.

**What readers are saying about
CZECHered PAST:**

"What a mesmerizing story! I can't believe I'm reading about my own father. Kudos for finding all the facts and putting them in order for a fascinating read."

"I found it intriguing, fascinating, and so many historical facts inter-woven in this drama. It's much more than an ordinary novel."

"I read one chapter and was hooked. Took the next day off work to finish this spellbinding book. Just couldn't put it down."

"Well written, factual and heartwarming. A must read. When's the next book coming out?"

"The story is captivating and details throughout create vivid images in the readers mind making one feel as though they were there. An easy read based on true life facts and characters I found extremely enjoyable. Truly a family treasure!"

Table of Contents

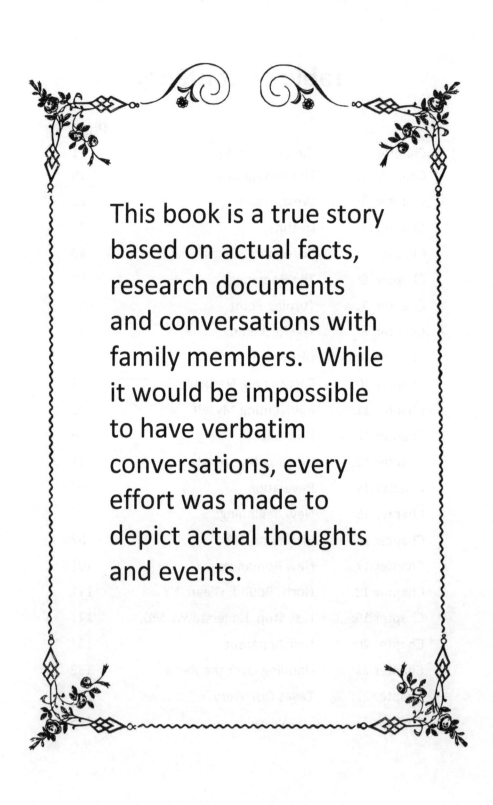

This book is a true story based on actual facts, research documents and conversations with family members. While it would be impossible to have verbatim conversations, every effort was made to depict actual thoughts and events.

THE CZECH TEXANS

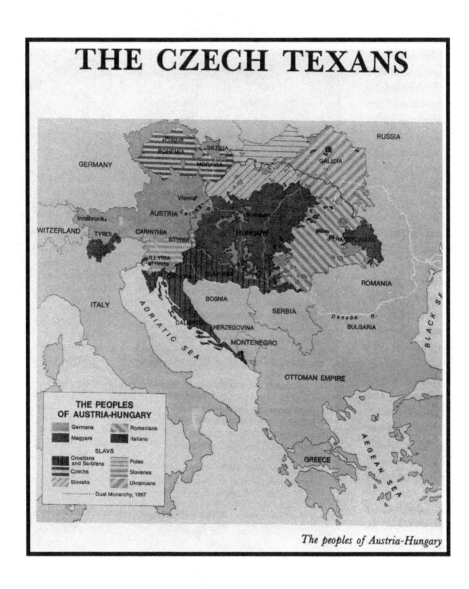

The peoples of Austria-Hungary

THE HAJEK FAMILY TREE

BARTOLOMEJ HAJEK
Born: Oct. 15, 1798 (Bohemia)
Married: Barbara Novotny 1820

MARTIN HAJEK
Born: Nov. 4, 1821 (Bohemia)
Married: Victoria Kulhanek
Died: Oct. 20, 1880 (Texas)

| Frank Herman Hajek 1855-1932 | William John Hajek 1860-1936 | Adolph Martin Hajek 1863-? | Marie Anna Hajek 1864-1946 | Antone Bartholomew Hajek 1867-1913 | **JOSEPH VICTOR HAJEK** Born: Mar 19, 1869 Died: Mar 3, 1956 | Paul Peter Hajek 1871-1952 |

EDWARD JOHN HAJEK 1890-1963

Joseph Emil Hajek 1894-1966

Mary Hajek Lednicky 1897-1955

Vilem Hajek 1893-1901

Julianna Hajek 1901-1902

Hettie Doris Hajek Drawbaugh 1923-2005

Marjorie Hajek 1921-1929

John H. Lednicky, Jr. 1924-2004

Jacqueline Patricia Hajek Werner 1927-

Juliette Hajek Taylor 1926-

RICHARD JOSEPH HAJEK 1931-

Norma Lee Hajek Daniel 1927-

Mary Jo Hajek Worthington 1928

Edward Wright Hajek 1929-2008

Wilbur Allen Hajek 1931-

Jeanene Claire Hajek Richardson 1933

Helen Ruth Hajek McDonald 1934-

Theodore Emil Hajek 1942-

Sharon Elizabeth Hajek Matzner 1945-

Chapter 1

HAGERSTOWN, MD

1963

I have only been dead 7 hours and already the closely guarded secret of my past has started to unravel. The secret life I was able to conceal from my family and friends for 50 years has begun to surface. Surface from the deep, dark recesses of my youth and years as a young man in Texas. Now that I am dead, yet not quite gone from this earth, I have to ask myself why was it so important to live a lie, a life of deception, a life far away from my hometown, relatives and tradition deeply steeped in the Czech culture. To drop dead of a heart attack while shaving at age 73 never entered my mind. Now I can only watch to see how my secret and my past life will be revealed. How long will it take them to put the pieces together, realizing what a complex man I was and how fate forever changed my life.

Most of the people involved and the Texas relatives with direct knowledge of actual events are also dead which leaves a cold trail for any inquisitive heir. But just like geology and archeology - everything is eventually dug up.

It was a cold, damp day on February 5, 1963 with traces of the latest snowfall still clinging to the trees. It had been a bone chilling winter in Hagerstown, MD with more snow than usual for this small town, 70 miles northwest of Baltimore. I thought today would be a typical day; rising early in the morning, grooming, donning my customary suit, vest and tie, my trademark rimless glasses, have breakfast with Hettie, my adoring wife of 40 years, and then off to the college. I, Edward J. Hajek, went everyday even though my son, Richard, was running the college by now. A heart attack a few years ago and subsequent episodes made us all realize that someone else had to take the reins at the school. Richard, the youngest of my three children, was a 1st Lieutenant in the Air Force and the whole family put enormous pressure on him to give up his military career for the Business College. Reluctantly he honored their wishes and came back to Hagerstown in 1955. How thoughtless of me to do to him exactly what had been done to me as a young man. Having family impose their wishes on a child's vocation that will forever alter the course of his life is the most selfish act of all.

The thud of my body hitting the cold tile bathroom floor caused Hettie to run from the kitchen to find me. She had the presence of mind to call Dr. Hoffman who lived just a block away on Oak Hill Avenue. He ran immediately to our house with his black medical bag in hand and began to work on me. It pained me to watch Hettie's trembling hands fumble with the black rotary phone as she dialed the number for Richard's home. He was stunned to receive a phone call from his mother so early in the morning and as soon as he heard her tearful voice, he knew something dreadful must have happened. His Mother was always the calm, rational one in the family so hearing her hysterical sobs spelled doom. She told Richard that I had fallen in the bathroom and suspected it was another heart attack, but was terrified because this time I was unresponsive.

Rushing to his parents' house several blocks away, Richard's mind raced with a swirl of unanswered questions regarding the school, his Dad's estate and how his beloved Mother would cope living alone. He got to their house on Potomac Avenue just in time to console his Mother as the doctor told them that this time I suffered a massive heart attack and passed away, nothing more could be done. A grief stricken Hettie crumbled into Richard's arms and wept for the love of her life. I had been her rock for over 40 years and now it was time to leave her until we meet again for all of eternity. Richard called his oldest sister, Doris, who also lived in Hagerstown, explaining what had transpired and asking her to come over immediately to help console their Mother. Later, the funeral home personnel prepared my body for transport to the funeral home and the family watched as they placed my lifeless body on the gurney and took me out the front door for the last time. Richard spent the next few hours making calls to his other sister, Jacqueline, who lived near Washington, DC, and to other family and friends. News of a sudden death is the most difficult to process but he did his best to console each of them. Jacqueline was in her third year of medical school at Georgetown University and had to be tracked down to the Georgetown Hospital's operating room where she was observing the morning's surgeries. She left immediately after a nurse broke the news to her about my passing. Meanwhile Richard was coming to grips with losing his Father and the knowledge that he was now solely responsible for the family business.

After a conversation with the Funeral Director, Richard returned to his parents' home to pick out a proper suit, shirt and tie for the funeral. As he looked through my dresser drawers for a pair of cuff links, he came across a stunning revelation: a rosary, an old prayer book and a book on the Catholic religion. Knowing his family was Methodist prompted him to call the number on the business card being used as a bookmark. It was the phone number for Father Dauch, of St. Joseph's Catholic

Church in Williamsport, just a few miles from Hagerstown. The Priest explained that I was in fact taking instruction to re-enter the Catholic faith. Richard presented the new found information to the family and they decided to bury me as a Catholic, figuring I would have wanted it that way.

I was a well-known businessman, having founded and owned The Hagerstown Business College for 25 years to date. I dealt with thousands of students and their parents, as well as serving in several community service clubs. This prompted the funeral home to prepare for a very large wake. Imagine the shock when friends and family entered The Minnich Funeral Home on Wilson Blvd. and found candles at the ends of my casket and a genuflecting rail. Most of the conversations began with "how sad to lose a pillar of the community" and quickly turned to "I thought the Hajek's were Methodist??" Most of the public was unaware that I never went to church while in Hagerstown or that I would drive my family there each Sunday morning, drop them off for church and Sunday school while I went to my office to work. It always felt like the college came first in my life, but nobody dared question my decisions.

Father Dauch recommended a small, private graveside service and burial to the family. His recommendation had a twofold purpose. The private graveside ceremony gave my family the closeness and closure they so desperately needed at this time of shock and sorrow. As my story unfolds, you will learn why a Requiem Mass would not have been permitted in the Catholic Church.

After the funeral Jacque and her husband, Hubert, went back to DC. Hettie told Doris, who had been staying with her Mother for a few days, to go back home. She felt she was strong enough now and had to start getting used to the idea of living alone. Richard and his young family went back to their lives saddened by the thought that I would never get to see their unborn son expected in a few months.

14

Chapter 2

THE IMMIGRANTS

1798

In reality there was much that family and friends never knew about me. I was born December 27, 1890 in Westphalia, located in western Falls County, Texas to Joseph Victor Hajek and Juliana Kolar Hajek. I was the eldest of five siblings however, as was common in those days, two died as very young children. We were a proud Czech family whose ancestors were from Bohemia, Czechoslovakia. We can trace our family back as far as Bartolomaj Hajek, born October 15, 1798 in Mahausch, Bohemia.

Czech Crest

He married Barbara Novetny in 1820. It was their son, Martin Hajek, born November 4, 1821 who made the decision to immigrate to America. Martin was born in the district of Netolice of Prachatice, in southwestern Czechoslovakia. My grandfather, Martin, like thousands of other oppressed Czechs fled the Moravia, Bohemia region in Czechoslovakia, now known as the Czech Republic. From 1620 until 1918 Austrians (Austro-Hungarian Empire) ruled the Czech people. During much of this time the Czechs were treated as a conquered people, their traditional customs, language and literature were subject to severe government restrictions. The Austrian army ruled with an iron fist, leaving young men with little or no choices in life. Their fate was to either join the Austrian army and face sure death or live in tyranny. That coupled with famine and religious persecution resulted in much suffering. They dreamed of a better life, a better future for their children, religious and political freedom and economic opportunity. People at the top of the social and economic order had no reason to leave. Those at the bottom, such as day laborers and impoverished unskilled factory workers didn't have the means to leave. It was the middle class--- skilled craftsmen, share-croppers and those owning 2-10 acres of land who became disenchanted. A strong and proud breed was left with one other avenue of escape - - - America. So, in the mid 1840's a group of them banded together and set out for an adventure of a lifetime.

The first group of Czechs arrived in America at Castle Garden, NY. These true pioneers made their way across this new country to central Texas where the land was cheap and fertile. They sent word back to Bohemia for the next wave of Czechs to sail for Galveston, Texas. Their theory was that it took too long to get through immigration at Castle Garden and far too long to traverse the 1,600 miles inland. Galveston was an ideal port of entry. It was a faster, more direct route to freedom and fertile farmland. The land in central Texas was black, rich land ideal for the farming heritage of their ancestors in Europe. The Blackland

Prairie Soil Region of Texas was a narrow strip of fertile blackland soils running north and south from Galveston to just north of Dallas. The newly immigrated Czechs tended to put down roots in Austin, Burleson and Fayette Counties. The first real Czech settlement was in Cat Springs, Austin County in 1847.

My Grandfather, Martin Hajek, was a strong-willed, hard-working man, determined to make something of his life. He married Terezie Hundl on October 28, 1851 in the Church of Nemcice in Bohemia. By 1854 he made the decision to leave

Nemcice Church

everything and everyone behind, taking his wife and daughter, Catherine, to the new dream of freedom in America. They had their passports issued in Prague on September 4, 1854, and stamped for travel on October 21, 1854. The three of them boarded the train that took them to Bremen, Germany. Their suitcases were packed with their most cherished possessions knowing they would never return to their homeland. Once in Bremen they made their way through the city to the port where they boarded the ship, Antoinette, which was scheduled to sail to London, then on to Galveston.

Port of Bremen, Germany

Once on board they found their crude accommodations, settled in and sought out other Czech passengers. Even though they knew they were doing the right thing for their future, they were sad to leave their Homeland. Meeting other Czechs and sharing stories of how their new lives in America would enrich their very existence helped tamp down the lump in their throats as the ship cast off and slipped out of the harbor. They all stood on deck and watched as the last glimpse of Europe faded into the horizon. There was no turning back now, only hopes, dreams and hard work would propel them the rest of their lives.

Trans-Atlantic Ship of the 1800's

It was a tumultuous 13 week voyage during winter months, causing many on board to become ill. Some succumbed to the hardships and passengers watched in horror as their loved ones were buried at sea. Conditions on the ships making the trans-Atlantic voyage in the 1800's were poor at best for those on board who could not afford first class accommodations. The food was bad, consisting of beans, bacon and wormy biscuits. The women would pick the worms out of the biscuits and did their best to make a meal edible. The voyage proved to be too long and difficult for Terezie and Catherine, as they both became gravely ill at the half way point. The Hajeks made friends with another couple onboard named Katzer. Sticking together was a strong Czech trait so it was only natural for Mrs. Katzer to care for both Terezie and Catherine.

Original Martin Hajek Passport

When the ship docked in Galveston, in February 1855, Martin showed his passport for the last time. This new land was now his home and there was no going back. They all stayed briefly in a Catholic shelter until they regained their land legs and adjusted to their new environment. He and a group of families bought provisions, a freight wagon and a strong team of oxen to get them to their ultimate destination. The men studied maps while onboard and decided to go further northwest than most of the other families. They traveled as far as Cat Springs, in

Austin County and Fayetteville, in Fayette County, Texas. After a much deserved rest and a tearful goodbye to their Czech friends, Martin, Terezie and Catherine struck out for their dream of a fertile farm and total freedom. The Czech families all settled within a tight radius east of Route 81 (now Route 35). They only had each other and sheer determination to rely on in their new land. Everything they needed to survive was created by their own hands. They used a barter system trading crops and food. They eventually published their own newspaper and established clubs. Their strong faith made them rich and that same faith will be passed down thru generations to come. There were approximately 700 Czechs in Texas by the Civil War; 9,200 by 1900 and 15,000 by 1910. In time over 250 Czech communities would spring up in Texas and at one time, Czech was the second largest spoken language.

Fayetteville

The journey to San Felipe took a bad turn when Terezie became ill again. She never did fully regain her strength from the ship-borne illness and died in San Felipe leaving Martin to care for Catherine who was now 3 years old. In a bizarre twist of fate, Martin's new friend, Mr. Katzer was killed in a hunting accident. When word of his demise reached Martin, he thought immediately of the kindness Victoria Katzer had shown his family. He visited Victoria often, tending to her farm chores and doing his best to console her in her time of grief. As the months passed their affections for each other grew, spurring Martin to ask her to become his wife. They were married November 26, 1855 in Frelsburg. It seemed like God had brought them together through that dreadful voyage, their combined grief and adapting to their new Czech community in Texas. They had seven children, the sixth being Joseph Victor, my father. In keeping with tradition, all the children were baptized Catholic.

Joseph Victor was born March 19, 1869 at their farm on the old Fayetteville/Columbus Road. He learned to work the land, to harness and drive teams of mules and horses that helped provide for the family. Czechs are known for their strong work ethic thus long hours were a normal way of life. Each family member was responsible for some facet of the farming operation. Teamwork was necessary for the survival and growth of the family. Times were tough in those days. Wood-burning stoves cooked their food and provided heat. Water was drawn from the well, cistern or creek by bucket and carried to the house. Farming equipment was crude, consisting of one-row plows or middle-busters pulled by oxen, horses or mules. Their families were large, caring and depended on each other. This closeness extended to distant relatives as well as friends. The Czech people were honest and reliable. Divorces were unheard of and family unity paramount. Ethics and principles were taught from an early age and the parents disciplined children who wavered from their strict rules. Czech characteristics were widely accepted in Texas because they were known as fun-loving, light-hearted people who loved to dance, sing and eat their ethnic food. They were industrious and excellent farmers, producing better crops than their non-Czech farming neighbors.

Tragedy struck the Hajek family on October 20, 1880 when Martin was killed by robbers in Frelsburg, Texas, 72 miles west of Houston, while delivering a load of lumber with his freight wagon. Martin was only 59 years old and was sorely missed by his wife, Victoria and their children. Victoria died just 2 years later at age 52. After the death of their parents, the boys took over the farm and provided for the family.

Young men were expected to marry women who were both Czech and Catholic. Intermarriages between Catholics and Protestants caused family conflicts. As a young man, Joseph, my father, was to marry Juliana Kolar, born in Lukovecka, Moravia. She was brought over to America to become his bride and keep true Czech bloodlines infused into the new Czech/American communities. They were wed January 9, 1890. Juliana spoke very little English and was a devout Catholic, attending Mass every day of her life. She and many other immigrants refused to learn to speak English. They were determined to live as Czechs even though they were in a new country. Tradition was everything to them and the old ways were tried and true.

Juliana Kolar Hajek's Wedding Day

Joseph Victor Hajek's Wedding Day
January 9, 1890

Chapter 3

WEST, TEXAS

1890

Joseph and Juliana grew to love each other in their "arranged marriage" and I was born two days after Christmas. My parents worked very hard and eventually bought a farm on the Aquilla creek. It had a modest two story frame farmhouse and a barn, but it was theirs. It was home for me, my brother Joseph, four years younger than I and my sister Mary, who was seven years my junior. She would be taught the art of cooking, canning, sewing and

Edward John Hajek, 1891

gardening. We all went to a primitive log cabin school when work on the farm didn't interfere. If the weather cooperated, we had classes under a big oak tree next to the school. Out of necessity, the crops came first so we boys were taught farming at an early age. The land was fertile, however the climate was harsh. The grueling Texas sun nearly fried me and my brother as we worked the fields. The sun would rise like a fireball. As the day progressed the hot, dry air was like opening an oven door and having the heat actually hurt your nostrils. Insects, dust storms, tornados and snowstorms all took its toll on the land, the animals, but most of all the people.

As we got older our responsibilities increased in number and difficulty. Harnessing four mules abreast and hitching them properly to the plow was a big chore for a youngster. It was imperative to get the heavy collars and pads over the tall horses' heads and settled perfectly on their shoulders to prevent chaffing and sores. The girth had to be adjusted properly permitting the harness to be secure yet allow the horses to breathe. The endless buckles and snaps from the breaching, the crupper and the traces would ensure that the plow or wagon being pulled would not be too close to the horses' hind legs and not run up against the horses' hocks when going downhill. Lastly the lines (not reins) had to be securely attached to the bridles and treaded back thru loops to the driver. The number of lines required was determined by the number of horses or mules being hitched. Depending on the experience of the team, some lines might only go to the lead or outside horses. Now that these beasts of burden were properly harnessed, I would have to decide if a single tree or double tree was required to hook-up to the object being pulled. I would line-drive the team to the wagon or plow and hitch-up, making one last check of all parts and buckles. It was always a relief to see Dad drive off with the team and know that he wouldn't have to worry about readjusting my mistakes.

We watched as our father skillfully turned the black soil and created straight furrows. Busting the uncultivated soil (hence the term "sod-buster" was given to farmers by the cattle ranchers) required enormous strength and perseverance. This job was much too difficult for young lads. Corn and cotton were our cash crops and we always had a hay field to sustain the livestock over the winter months. The rich soil grew a mixture of prairie grasses producing two cuttings per year. Czech farmers baled all their hay, believing it was better preserved than the hay stacks other farmers made. Joseph and I both hated working in the cotton fields. Picking cotton until our hands bled from the prickly pods convinced us both that we would never grow cotton when "we" ran the family farm.

If we weren't tending the fields, we would fix fences, repair buildings, harness and tools. Cutting trees for fire wood was a regular duty. Dad selected the trees and Joseph and I cut them down with the cross-cut saw. Next we would slap a logging chain around the trunk, hook it up to the team of mules and drag them back to the house. We boys could saw them with the cross-cut saw, relying on each-others strength to push and pull the saw at the precise second. The saw cut as if going through butter when we got the rhythm going just right. Dad had to split the hard, green wood -- too much for a lad. He would split the firewood so fast that it kept us busy stacking it and keeping up with him. As I got older, he taught me his tricks to splitting wood. I gradually began to get the hang of it and could relieve him once in a while. We all worked hard, but Dad saw that twice a week we "men" would go hunting. It was cherished quality time for just the three of us. Rabbits, squirrels, pheasants and deer were plentiful but we never shot more than our family could eat.

Dad eventually bought another farm near a town called West, just south of Fort Worth. He was one of the founding fathers of this town, helping to develop a strong Czech community. The main road around West is still "Hajek Road", named for my father. To this day it is known as Little Czechoslovakia, famous for its kolaches, a delectable pastry. Kolaches are a circular tart made of special double-risen dough whose center is topped or filled with poppy seed sauce, peaches or other fruits. The small town was originally called Bold Springs but had its name changed to West in 1881. It was named after a young man, Thomas M. West, from Kentucky who came to Texas to work on a ranch in Freestone County. He saved his money for three years and then purchased land near the mouth of

Cottonwood Creek, about three miles east of Bold Springs. There he started a cattle ranch until the outbreak of the Civil War.

Bold Springs

Texans wanting to stay out of the war voted overwhelmingly in February 1861 to secede from the Union only to watch as their state joined the Confederacy in March. The four-year conflict took the lives of many and touched every family in some way. Texas escaped much of the terrible destruction of the war as Union troops never managed to invade and occupy the state's interior. Nevertheless, Texans paid a huge price for the war, primarily in terms of lives lost and families ruined at home. The only Texans who benefited significantly from the war were the state's approximately 200,000 black slaves who gained freedom at the close of the conflict in 1865.

From 1861 to 1865, Thomas West served in the 19th Texas Cavalry (Confederacy) and achieved the rank of Captain. After an honorable discharge, West returned to his McLennan County ranch and married Martha Adams Steele, a Civil War widow. Mr. West purchased 260 acres in 1872 which later became a significant part of the city when the Missouri, Kansas, Texas (MKT) Railroad would come through his tract of land. Thomas West went on to become founder of West's first bank, the West Furniture Co., and served as postmaster and general store operator.

The town of West soon developed into a dominant commercial center in the area. This railroad-centered community was incorporated in 1892 with a population of approximately 1,000. West continued to boom and by the turn of the century the population had doubled. It was also famous for Nemecek's Meat Market and Joseph Janek's Saloon. Story has it that my father would stand at the end of the bar most evenings, drink one beer and then leave for home.

WEST STATION — 1895 — PINE STREET

West was the perfect place for our family's farm. It had fertile dark soil with cottonwood trees separating the fields. When not totally flat, gentle rolling hills barely obscured the view of the horizon. The first settlers had to clear all this land of trees and the dense mesquite bushes. The hard mesquite limbs were an excellent source of wood for cook stoves and fireplaces giving off an intense heat.

Dad was a handsome man with a strong build, steel eyes and a full head of hair that turned white prematurely. His tanned, leathered skin, mustache and shock of white hair made him take on the appearance of a "true Texan". Strong as he was, he somehow became gravely ill around 1904. The doctor was not sure he could save him so Juliana prayed to God that "If He would spare her husband, *they would send their eldest son into the priesthood*".

That is the fateful day that my life was changed forever. My Father lived. I was 14 years old. I went from being a small town farm boy, steeped in the simple ways of hunting, fishing, working the land and tending the livestock to being sent away to a seminary on the east coast of Texas, where I was destined to become a Priest.

Most Czechs were Catholic but my Mother was almost obsessed with her religion. As if going to mass every day wasn't enough, she would make Joseph and me ride mules into town several times a week to get meat from Nemecek's Meat Market and take it to

the Priest and Nuns. Priests were not paid a large salary by the Diocese. To compensate, parishioners were expected to give the Priest prime cuts of meat every time they butchered.

During the turn of the century it was tradition for the eldest son to do whatever his parents chose for him as an appropriate vocation. These vocations were almost always close to their home and followed the fathers' line of work. Therefore, I always assumed I would take over the farm for my father and care for the family. Most of my friends were to assume roles as farmers, shopkeepers or tradesmen. How could it be that I was to give up everything I knew, leave my home, stifle my yearnings as a young man to date local maidens, court, marry and propagate the land with MY own children and MY own name. How could any parent ask *all that* of a child? Weren't Priests to receive a special calling from God?

The die was cast!!! *A holy promise is a holy promise.* I believed in God, I was a true Catholic and I always honored my parents, so maybe it **was** my destiny to be a Priest and I just didn't know it yet.

Regardless, I couldn't keep myself from wondering what my life would have been like as a normal member of the Czech community. Apparently my good looks caught the eyes of the young ladies at community gatherings. I had Raven black hair, high cheek bones on a face tanned by the Texas sun. Even at this young age my body was chiseled from the heavy lifting and endless work on the farm.

Our family attended a wedding where my brother and I got to size up the girls while they did the same to us. Czech weddings are elaborate by tradition and it was the perfect place to mingle with young folks and catch up on the news.

A traditional Czech wedding required careful preparation. The young couple rented land on which to live and farm after their wedding day. Feeding the many guests required her parents to raise additional chickens, turkeys, a hog and a calf. Two of the groomsmen would wear their Sunday best and ride around from house to house extending formal invitations. A few days before the wedding, friends gathered to help with preparing food and seating arrangements. Not only did they have to prepare food for the wedding feast, but also for the guests' trip back home. Numerous kegs of beer, or pivo in Czech, were provided as beer drinking was an art in the Czech culture.

The groom could not see his bride in her wedding dress until everyone gathered at the church parlor. There, a man called the "starosta" stepped forward and presented the bride to the groom. He admonished the groom to be kind, gentle and worthy, and the bride to be moral, obedient and submissive. Both were told to honor their parents. Next was the procession to the sanctuary for a formal wedding Mass. After the ceremony everyone returned to the bride's home. A collection was taken to buy a cradle for their first born. Then came the virtual orgy of eating, drinking, dancing and visiting. It required great stamina to survive a Czech wedding, but few invitations were ever turned down.

Czech wedding in Fayetteville

Typical Czech Wedding

Hajek Family before Edward was sent away, 1904
(Left to right) Mary, Joseph Victor, Edward,
Juliana, Joseph Emil

On the way home from the wedding, my mind drifted
between wondering what the groom's wedding night would be
like, to my days as a boy on the farm, working with the animals.
Breeding season always intrigued me as a boy. Watching the
bulls mount the cows in the fields or taking our mares to the
neighbors' stallion to be bred gave me a natural thrill. The force
with which the studs mounted the mares, slamming his front

hooves against her sides, thrusting his 26 inch erect penis into his willing recipient left a lasting impression in the mind of a teenage boy. The stallion would bite the crest of her neck to maintain his balance while heaving relentlessly until his job was done. I noticed that the older I got, the more it excited me as hormones raged through my teenage body. I couldn't help but wonder how it would feel when I had sex for the first time with my wife on our wedding night. Would I overtake her like the stallion or would I be gentle, softly nibbling at her neck, long tender kisses, lovingly stroking her gorgeous body. The thought of never experiencing the most natural act of manhood almost made me sick to my stomach. Was I going to be strong enough to suppress my natural urges and give up what I considered a normal life for my parents and for God?

Chapter 4

DESTINY

1904

Priesthood was a long way off, as it required 4 years of college and 4 years of seminary, plus I still had three years of high school to complete first. Nevertheless, in the fall of 1904, at the tender age of fourteen, I was put on a train and sent to St. Mary's Seminary in La Porte, Fort Bend County, near Houston. I had never been away from home before and found watching the scenery pass by helped ease my anxiety. I was amazed to see the changes in the terrain and the soil. The land looked like it had sand mixed in it, explaining why the coastal Bermuda grasses thrived here. The ranchers depended on its resilience for their herds, knowing that it did well in draught then greened up faster than other grasses. This land was a far cry from the rich, black soil back home.

The fear of being away from home was magnified by the fact that I was being sent to La Porte near Galveston. Just 4 years ago, in 1900, a catastrophic hurricane slammed into the coastal towns at night leaving thousands dead and wide-spread destruction. I was told that La Porte was a small town less than 70 miles north of Galveston. Having never seen the ocean, I was secretly terrified to live so close to it. True, Galveston was located on a spit of land, actually classified as an island and La Porte was on the coast of the mainland. However, as a boy the proximity was entirely too close to ease my fears.

Galveston grew from a small settlement into one of the wealthiest cities in the country. Its natural deep water channel made it the most important seaport in Texas. Trains carried cargo to and from the port, then heavy laden ships traveled across the seas. Over 70% of the nation's cotton crop passed through this port and over 1,000 ships called on the port annually. Galveston was home to 37,000 residents and its wealth and prosperity was home to numerous firsts in the state such as first electricity and the first telephones.

Galveston beaches were known for their shallow waters, perfect for bathers to wade safely offshore several yards and enjoy what was considered therapeutic bathing in the Gulf. Unfortunately those same characteristics would lead to its demise. The "Great Storm" of September 8, 1900 was the largest natural disaster to hit the country. Galveston took the brunt of the 135 mph winds and 15 foot storm surge. The local meteorologist, Isaac Cline, tracked the storm with his crude equipment, fearing the worst. He rode his horse up and down the beach pleading with people to head for higher ground and to evacuate at least 3 blocks of the city. Unfortunately there was no higher ground as the highest house in the city was at 8 or 9 feet elevation. By the time night fell, the entire island was under water. The wood framed homes, hotels and businesses collapsed and as the surge continued, a wall of debris described as at least two stories high pushed across the island. Everything in its path was destroyed. Out of the city's 37,000 people, 6,000 lost their lives in the darkness. In his memoirs, Cline described the terror of that night as he huddled with his family, and the bewilderment of seeing the total devastation the next morning.

Ironically, "The next day was warm and sunny, just like the weather for which Galveston is known".

The 1900 Storm - Galveston

Men Standing in Ruins

Market Shops

Four Blocks Flattened

Wall of Debris

Bodies Lined-Up

Like everyone in Texas, I heard stories of how those 31,000 people fortunate enough to survive the storm set out to recover bodies, bury their dead and rebuild their city. Pictures taken after the storm showed empty streets -- no people, no animals, no trees -- only piles of debris that buried families beneath. I heard that the stench of decaying bodies, fish and other animals rotting in the streets was unimaginable. The rebuilding of Galveston was to include raising the elevation of the town 16 feet and building a formidable seawall. Like the rest of my future, I would have to put my fear of living next to the ocean in Gods' hands.

St. Mary's Seminary, was originally the Sylvan Beach Hotel, damaged by the 1900 hurricane. It was purchased in 1901 by the Diocese of Galveston under the direction of Bishop Nicholas A. Gallagher and restored. It was the dream of Bishop Gallagher that each diocese have its own seminary. Pope Leo XIII sent his special blessing to the new school in these words: "I give my special blessings to you, that you prosper, and go forward to produce strong and religious men". During its early period it was under the direction of the Basilian Fathers. Enrollment increased yearly forcing the lay students to move into a cement structure added in 1908. The old hotel building was hereafter for the exclusive use of seminarians and faculty. In 1911 the Basilians withdrew and diocesan Priests took over the administration.

The seminary also served as a boarding high school and college for boys and

THE OLD ST. MARY'S SEMINARY, LA PORTE, TEXAS

St. Mary's Seminary, La Porte, Texas

young men. The school was over-powering to me with the main building five stories high. Each floor had a porch or balcony running the length and width of the structure allowing access to the dorm rooms and classrooms. It had a spacious grassy area in front used for concerts, plays and occasional baseball game. The whole place bustled with activity by boys in their knickers and girls in long, flowing dresses and big hats. A small number of girls attended the high school and then left for their college education. It was a genteel era with no thoughts of impropriety. St. Mary's was to be my home for the next eleven years, so I told myself that I had to adjust and be thankful for being given the best education a young man could ask for.

I found myself living a strange new existence. No longer did I rise in the mornings to face endless hours of physical labor. Instead I dressed in a suit and tie, considered appropriate school attire, ate a generous breakfast with my classmates before going to morning prayers in the Chapel. The rest of the day was consumed with a heavy class load of topics completely foreign to my log cabin schooling back in West. A letter from my parents with a picture of them and my brother, Joe, only compounded my being homesick and feeling out of place.

Family Portrait. Joseph Victor, Juliana, and Joseph Emil Hajek circa 1905.

To compensate, I made friends with an older gentleman named Patrick Fitzgerald, a Civil War veteran who was the school's caretaker. Everyone called him "Mr. Fitz". He lived in the barn with "Maude" a fast trotting black mare, the buggy, milk cows and some chickens. He was the school's yard man, barn man, milkman, kitchen aid, and official "cheer-up" guy. He was a natural buffer between the homesick youngsters and this lonesome place. I think we became friends because of my farming background, giving us lots to talk about and he allowed me to help him with minor farm chores when I had some free time. I hated to admit it after those years of hard work on the farm, but it felt good to hold a pitch fork and clean out stalls. We got into deep conversations while fixing fence, and bared our souls to each other. He appreciated the help because the

41

academia of the Seminary didn't understand that it took two people to fix wire fencing: one to hold the wire-stretchers and one to nail the wire to the post. It was a comfort just to know Mr. Fitz was there. On drab rainy evenings, since there were no recreational facilities, except to play dominoes, table games and ping-pong, he entertained the brood with yarn after yarn about Vicksburg, the Civil War, the railroad through Arizona and fighting Indians out hunting for scalps. He was one of the many newly inducted Confederate soldiers sent to Indian Territories further west to control the Indians so the already trained soldiers could fight the Union back East.

Mr. Fitz told stories about the importance of the Battle of Galveston. The Union launched a blockade on Galveston Bay on July 2, 1861 with the arrival of U.S.S. South Carolina. This screw-propelled steamer made several quick captures of slower sailing vessels trying to break through the blockade. The blockade forced the Confederacy to transport their cash crop of cotton into Mexico and then shipped to overseas markets.

On January 1, 1863, Maj. Gen. John B. Magruder crossed over the bridge from the mainland to Galveston at 1:00 AM launching a bold attack to recapture the city from Union troops. Just as Magruder assumed, Union troops were recovering from a night of New Year's Eve celebrations. He moved his infantry into the city under the cover of darkness and not only reclaimed Galveston, but also captured the famed Union ship, Harriet Lane and three Union transports. It was such a decisive victory that the Union never attempted to reclaim their position and Galveston port remained in the hands of the Confederacy until the end of the war. Mr. Fitz was a fountain of knowledge and had a gift for storytelling, which made history come alive. To keep that many boys spellbound for hours was truly an accomplishment.

I met other Czech lads which greatly reduced my anxiety level. It became evident early on, that speaking Czech was frowned upon. We obeyed the rules, but reverted to our native tongue when others were not present. Through sheer persistence, we were able to convince the College Board members that speaking Czech would be a useful tool when preaching to the parishes throughout Texas with large concentrations of Czech settlers. They finally agreed to add a class teaching the Czech language. I was asked to be the instructor of this class while I was still a student myself. **I think that experience is where I developed my love for teaching.** For years I was president of the Czech Literary Club and was instrumental in publishing a Czech newsletter for the school, as well as producing plays in Czech for the student body. I quickly established myself as a leader and a person who loved to teach.

Even with my academic achievements, seminary was going to be more difficult for me. It was frustrating listening to fellow future Priests or Candidates talk about how they were "called" into the ministry and how abstinence came natural to them. Apparently, *not* giving in to the natural urges of a young man didn't bother them. I never once uttered my opinion or shared my nagging questions for fear of appearing weak or uncertain of my intentions to become a priest. I wondered if I was destined

Young Seminarians and Students at St Mary's
Edward J. Hajek: Second Row from the back, far right

to a life of battling my internal conflict of desire vs. duty, living with the devil on one shoulder and an angel on the other.

I wondered how the seminary found enough young men willing to become priests. I later learned in my classes that *the Holy Spirit will call forth in abundance men who are called to both the priestly ministry and celibacy.* We were taught that celibacy, purity and chastity were gifts from God, given to chosen men, enabling their urges to be taken from them. I wasn't the only fourteen year old boy at St. Mary's as it was a common practice to recruit at a young age. However, I did learn that I <u>was</u> the only boy there who did not receive a true "calling" from God. Unlike them, I was the only one <u>told</u> that I was going to be a Priest.

In seminary our coursework consisted of two years of Philosophy followed by a four to six year course in Theology. Other subjects were: Logic, Psychology, Metaphysics, Physics, Chemistry, Physiology, Scripture, Church History, English Literature, Rhetoric, Latin and Greek. The Theology course also included Dogma, Moral and Pastoral Theology, Canon Law, Liturgy and Church Music. It was a heavy course-load for a farm boy but I thrived on learning. The Latin and Greek was a skill that would serve me later in life, unbeknownst to me then. I finished my classical course in 1910,

Edward J. Hajek, Seminarian

philosophy in 1912 and theology in 1915.

At the conclusion of seminary training, priest candidates were ordained. My ordination occurred during a Mass celebration on June 18, 1915, at the age of 25. This ceremony is sometimes referred to as, "Receiving the Sacrament of Holy Orders". Two other men were also ordained that day, (Fathers Ignatius Valenta and Joseph Hanak). It was a grand event held at St. Mary's Seminary during the annual retreat for the Priests of the Diocese, presided over by the Bishop himself, bedecked in his white and gold dalmatic robe. The three of us were ordained sub-deacons on Wednesday, June 16; deacons on Thursday the 17th; and Priests on Friday the 18th.

The church was full of parishioners, visiting Priests, choir boys, Nuns and Priest candidates with years left in their training but eager to see the spectacle. My heart leaped with joy when I glanced to the right and saw my family in the pew. They wanted to surprise me by all being here to share in this momentous occasion. I had not heard from them after sending the invitation from the seminary. However, I could not imagine my mother missing this blessed event since she was taking full credit for my success at St. Mary's. To hear her talk, she was making the supreme sacrifice, not me.

I was almost swept away between the reverence and the grandeur of the service which was about to begin. The service would last nearly 3 hours due to the sanctity of the event and the pomp and circumstances associated with the rituals in the church in 1915. It was to be a moving, holy experience.

The candidates were dressed in their Alb (white robes). The organ played as the boys' choir sang softly in the background from the balcony, and a feeling of reverence washed over the sanctuary as their voices echoed throughout the ornate rafters and painted ceiling. We marched into the church behind the ranking Bishops and Priests with our hands folded in humility. It was almost magical listening to the presiding Priest chant the service, with the choir boys echoing his chants. I never felt closer to God than I did at that moment. As I knelt in front of the Bishop, dressed in his full garb of robes, hat, and incense swirling around me, I felt him place his hands on my head causing me to receive the Holy Spirit. Next he gently rubbed holy water across my palms and folded my hands together between his, saying "Peace be with you", signifying that my hands were pure to go forward and do God's will. Then I lay face down on the floor before him, arms outstretched like the cross, signifying the death of my old being. I listened to the Litany of the Saints and for him to declare me reborn into my new identity. I felt myself totally submitting to God, totally absorbing God's grace and love. I left that service feeling that perhaps *I really was destined to be a Priest and promised myself that I would do my best to honor God and his work.*

After receiving my vestments and Roman collar, I spent the rest of the day with my family before their train departed for West.

The vestments were an intricate part of the Catholic service and considered a Priestly duty. It was actually considered a sin to forget one of the eight layers or one of the prayers said while donning each garment.

1. Cassock: Black floor length robe.
2. Amice: White rectangular cloth with strings going over the head and tucked around the Roman collar.
3. Alb: White floor length robe.
4. Cincture: Rope tied around the waist to protect their loins. Praying for sexual purity and celibacy.
5. Stole: Color of the day, signifying the authority of the Priest through Jesus Christ.
6. Chasuble: Large garment open on both sides, some plain, others ornate with gold.
7. Manipole of Tears: Cloth worn over left arm signifying the Priest weeping for our sins.
8. Biretta: A black, three-cornered hat with a pom-pom on top.

While wearing all these garments, a priest had a mystic, almost celestial look about him. He would swing the incense and chant the prayers offering the assurance of peace to his flock.

Each priest had to be skilled at the Rubrics. These were the instructions in red on how to say mass, even down to how to hold his fingers. Every priest carried this manual that was filled with prayers for every occasion or circumstance. This Prayer Book became an integral part of each priest, almost an appendage of his being. He was also expected to adhere to Canon Law which was strict and unforgiving in the early 1900's.

Initially I thought eleven years was a long time to learn a trade, but having just completed my ordination, I realized that it took every single day of instruction to learn the faith and rituals that went along with it.

Priest in Amice

Priest in Alb

Priest adjusting the cincture

Vestments

Priest putting Maniple on left arm

Priest with the Stole

Priest in Chasuble is now completely Vested

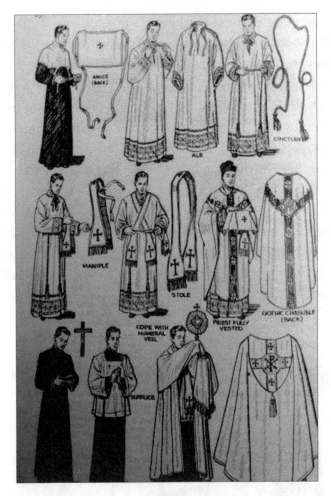

Vestments

The day after my ordination, I was assigned to be the first Priest of Rosenberg, Texas at Our Lady of the Holy Rosary Church. It was completed and dedicated in 1912 by the Most Reverend Bishop N. A. Gallagher of Galveston. Rosenberg was 59 miles southwest of Houston, thus part of the Galveston-Houston Diocese.

Chapter 5

ROSENBERG, TEXAS

1915

Rosenberg seemed like a natural fit for me as it was a town surrounded by Czech families who were buying up uncultivated acreage. It was a small town in Fort Bend County, incorporated in 1902. By 1914 it had its own Volunteer Fire Department boasting ownership of a two-wheel hand-drawn hose reel with 500 feet of hose. It was pulled to the fires by 10 or 12 men. There were 56 businesses such as banks, land development firms, merchants, doctors and lawyers. The dirt streets bustled with horses and buggies, ladies with long dresses and parasols, and cowboys from the local ranches. All the horses were unnerved by the occasional new-fangled automobile owned by only the most prominent businessmen. The first electrical generating plant was built in 1912, providing electricity to the town, however farm families didn't get the much needed, prized energy service until after World War I.

Up to this point in time, Father Montreal visited once a month to celebrate Holy Mass and administer the Holy Sacraments. Services were held in a Hall owned by a town resident. When the congregation grew, he decided it was time to build a church.   Rosenberg's first church cost an amazing

Kostel Panny Marie Růžencové

Our Lady of the Holy Rosary Church, Rosenberg, Texas

Vnitřek nového kostela v Rosenberg

Father Edward J. Hajek served 1915-17

$1,200 to build, a tidy sum in those days. Father Montreal died suddenly while on a mission tour in South America, thus creating an opening for me at the time I was ordained.

It is now 1915 and the congregation of Our Lady of the Holy Rosary church had grown expediently. The town anxiously awaited their first Priest, the newly ordained, Father Edward J. Hajek. I was eager to assume my new duties and minister to

Rosenberg's people. I was also assigned to celebrate Mass twice a month at St. Michael's church in Needsville, a small town approximately 10 miles away. Sometimes I felt guilty experiencing the joy and fulfillment of my current life situation knowing that young men my

Father Edward J. Hajek

age were dying in the "war to end all wars" - - World War I. I could only pray for those brave lads. Pray for their safe return or for their souls. I felt doubly guilty knowing that my kid brother, Joseph, was in the Navy aboard a cruiser overseas. I prayed daily for him, but was somewhat relieved that he was on a ship and not freezing in some foreign foxhole.

To think that this dreadful war of nations was ultimately triggered by the assassination of Archduke Franz Ferdinand of

Austria, heir to the Austro-Hungarian throne and his wife, Duchess Sophie on June 28, 1914. A bomb was thrown into their auto but missed. Undaunted, they continued their visit in Sarajevo, Bosnia only to be shot and killed a short time later by a lone assassin, Gavrilo Princip, a Bosnian Serb. The Austro-Hungarian Empire declared war on Serbia that same day.

Tensions escalated across Europe until August 1, 1914 when Germany declared war on Russia.

WWI American Soldiers Resting

On February 4, 1915 the Germans began unrestricted submarine warfare against merchant vessels, striking fear in all nations. Then on May 7, a German U-boat sank the British liner, Lusitania. Italy declared war on Austria-Hungary on May 23 and by August 5 the

WWI American Soldiers Examining a Crashed French Airplane

Germans occupied Warsaw. Trench warfare was responsible for thousands of deaths in the harsh Russian winters.

By late March, 1917,

Germany sank four more U.S. merchant ships, which resulted in President Wilson appearing before the U.S. Senate on April 2 seeking approval to go to war. Two days after the Senate voted 82 to 6 to declare war against Germany, the U.S. House of Representatives endorsed the declaration by a 373 to 50 vote. With that, America entered World War I on April 6, 1917. President Wilson pledged to remain neutral when the war first erupted in 1914, however, the loss of US ships and lives forced his hand.

Even though Rosenberg was a small town, the war eventually took a toll on its families. As their Priest I offered condolences, prayers and the assurance that they would be with their sons again in Heaven. Most of the poor lads were blown to bits or buried in Europe, so conducting the actual funeral was unnecessary. Almost 117,000 US military gave their lives trying to obtain world peace.

When I arrived in Rosenberg, the house provided for the Priest was some distance from the church as it sat out alone, near the Brazos River. Its solitude was a respite from the responsibilities of the congregation, their confessions and the toll of the war. Occasionally in the evening, I would take a swim and it reminded me of my happy days on the farm. My brother, Joe, and I learned to swim in the nearby Aquilla creek after a hot day's work.

The trek to and from the church was a daunting challenge for me through all kinds of weather. I was still using a horse and carriage to visit parishioners. My farm upbringing made it easy for me to care for the horse and hitch-up the carriage. A decision was made in time to trade that property for a two story house with two lots next to the church. The parish added $1,000 in the deal.

I was adjusting nicely to the town, my new duties and the church members. Letters from home let me know how proud my parents were of me in my new role as Priest. In time I was permitted to visit my home for a few days. The Sunday I preached in our family church, Church of the Assumption, while visiting my parents in West, was probably the happiest day of my Mother's life. She had everything she ever wanted - - - her healthy husband, her church, and her "holy promise" Priest son. To a packed church, I preached the entire service in Czech that day in honor of my mother. Normally the church in Rosenberg preferred Latin, with some Czech mixed into the services. It was a glorious family day, with my second cousin, Victor, Jr. serving as my altar boy. Family and friends told me it was one of the most reverent Masses they ever attended and that I had a beautiful voice for chanting. I must admit it was gratifying to be appreciated by my family and hometown after all the years of preparation.

Church of the Assumption, West, Texas

Apparently there was one more thing Mother wanted. While visiting West, my brother, Joseph told me that Mother was pressing to sell the farm and move into West so she could be closer to the church for her daily Mass. I received word later in 1917 that Dad had in fact sold the farm and bought a house at 303 Davis Street in West. Dad was only 48 years old and had lots of farming years left in him, but he loved Mother and did his best to make her happy.

Dad became a partner in the West Furniture Company and Undertaking establishment. He remained active in this business until 1939 when he retired at age 70. Dad always kept a few chickens in his back yard and would now have to be content sitting on the porch listening to the mockingbirds, the Texas state bird. Mother would continue to keep her customary "tidy" house and make her famous homemade noodles. Soup was an important part of the noon time meal, so Czech women rolled-out, paper thin egg noodle dough. It was a common sight in a Czech home to see this dough spread out on a table or draped over chairs. After drying, the sheet of dough was rolled and cut into strips, to be used in various kinds of noodle soups.

When I arrived in Rosenberg I learned that they were also in need of a School Superintendent so I offered my services. I assured the town that I was fully capable of maintaining my

Edward J. Hajek, School Superintendent, Rosenberg, Texas
Last Row, Center

Priestly duties and overseeing the school based on my teaching experience at St. Mary's Seminary. I loved the new challenge and felt fulfilled back in a teaching role.

Of all my duties as a Priest, I found administering to the sick and conducting funerals to be the hardest. To connect with the parishioners, watch them suffer and eventually die saddened my soul. I tried my best to never let these feelings show as that would surely weaken my position as their spiritual leader.

During the winter of 1916 and 1917, I was called to the home of a prominent town leader to offer prayer for their 18 year old daughter. Her name was Evelina. She developed a bad case of pneumonia and the doctor wasn't sure she would weather this ordeal. Her high fever and nagging cough took its toll on her petite body. Each day for two weeks I came to their home, a stately two-story brick with pillars on the front porch, all signs of the wealth which she had become accustomed to as a child. I sat with her reading scripture, prayed for her recovery from my Pastoral Book of Prayers and granted her absolution. Then I consoled the family with assurance that God was watching over her.

As she lie in her bed in a semi-conscious state, I would end my prayers, then with the back of my thumb make the mark of the cross on her forehead and palms of her hands as an act of absolution. In time, I found myself begging God to spare her, not realizing that I had become attached to this beautiful woman. Her skin was so fair, her eyes green, having caught a glimpse the few times I saw them open. Her hair was auburn and fell softly against her shoulders. I fought the urges flickering through my mind and focused on my duties, but each time I touched her forehead or hand I lingered a little longer.

Until one evening when I was alone with her and my urges overpowered my common sense. I finished my prayer, made the mark of the cross on her forehead and found the side of my hand gently sliding down the side of her face.

To my amazement, she opened her eyes and looked directly into mine. I jerked my hand away and resumed my Priestly stance hoping that she had not felt my touch. Trembling overcame my body as she took my hand and kissed it softly.

"Father Hajek, thank you for being there all those days and nights. I knew when you were there and it was so reassuring when I felt the pull between my Heavenly home and my earthly bounds. Are my parents home?"

"I am so happy to see you alert and talking. You had us all worried for two weeks."

We spoke for a short time awaiting the arrival of her parents back home from a town meeting. When we heard the front door close, I met them at the top of the stairs and shared the wonderful news. We all said a prayer of thanks for what appeared to be a turning point in her recovery.

"I will let myself out", I said. "Be back in the morning to see if she's still making progress. God bless you all."

Driving back to the rectory I prayed that her parents had not detected my trembling hands or the look of guilt on my face. That night I fell to my knees beside my bed begging for forgiveness. Forgiveness for succumbing to earthly thoughts and feelings. Forgiveness for not upholding my Priestly vows. Our God blessed us with free will, but with free will comes hard choices.

Edward's Pastoral Book of Prayers

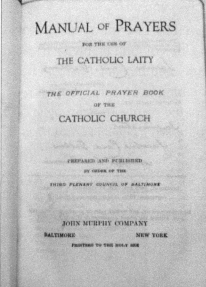

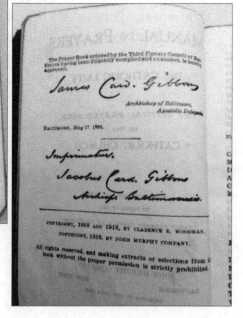

Chapter 6

THE ROMANCE

1917

The next day after our Matin Service, morning prayers, I went back to see how Evelina was doing. It was a crisp morning, but the sun seemed to shine brighter than I had ever witnessed. I spoke to her Father as he passed me on the front sidewalk. He was off to his local business, which was prospering, as was all of Rosenberg. Her Mother eagerly answered my knock, bursting to tell me that her daughter had a restful night and actually ate some breakfast. She took my coat and hat, instructing me to go upstairs to see for myself.

I tapped on Evelina's bedroom door and entered at her beckoning. She was sitting up in bed for the first time with the bright sunlight streaming through the window and dancing on her hair. It was refreshing to see signs of color in her cheeks and a smile on those pretty lips. For a while we just talked like two young people would about the weather and what she had missed in town during the weeks of her illness. It wasn't until we heard her mother's footsteps coming close to the door that we reverted to our *proper* roles as Priest and patient.

As the days and weeks progressed, my official visits could have ceased. Finding a plausible excuse to stop by her home was the trick, followed by my customary pangs of guilt and prayers for forgiveness. I knew it was wrong, but I had never felt more alive. What hold did this woman have over me? Is this how love felt? The fleeting moments with Evelina made me happy, made me feel whole, made me feel like a man. It worried me that I was nine years her senior, but girls married much younger than her eighteen years of age. Her maturity surpassed her age, possibly a result of her sophisticated upbringing.

Evelina was well-known in Rosenberg for both her academic achievements at school and for her charitable work at church and in the community. If something needed to be done, Evelina was the first person people approached. She had an air of confidence about her that blended perfectly with her cheerful disposition. Even at her young age, she knew how to organize a group of people or an event. Evelina possessed a gentle spirit and helping people was her true passion.

The long awaited Texas spring was finally here and Rosenberg residents were out and about. Flower pots were planted and placed strategically on the front porches and perennials were beginning to bloom in the flower beds. Children and their dogs were playing in the front yards, now bright with green grass and flowers. Bluebonnets and Indian Paint Brush were blooming in the endless flat fields making them appear to touch the sky. They formed a sorbet of colors shouting God's splendor in all creation. Understandingly, the Blue Bonnets were just named the official State flower in 1901. Farmers were busy preparing their fields for planting and the whole world seemed to come alive. The church was also busy preparing for its annual Spring Bazaar. Ladies were cooking their favorite dishes and fixing tables of dry goods which they knitted or crocheted during the long winter days hoping to sell them at the bazaar. A few local artist displayed their paintings and pottery, waiting for someone who couldn't resist taking them home.

Evelina was strong and vibrant by now and gladly took the role as coordinator of the bazaar. As I walked into the social room the night before the festivities were to begin, I found her working alone.

"And what keeps you here so late?"

As she looked up and saw me, a warmth swept over both of us.

"I'm double checking all the tables, the list of food to be sold and what to feed the volunteers from the church kitchen. I thought you would be gone for the day."

We just stood there looking at each other for what seemed like an eternity. Since her illness, we had a few conversations, long, lingering glances across the room and even an occasional squeeze of the hand. However brief, each one drew us closer together affirming that we were in fact, falling in love. There seemed to be a special bond between us, an easy, natural feeling even when we were simply talking. We were young and OH how we longed to just hold each other. We were eager to experience the tenderness that both of us could only imagine until now. Our feelings for each other were deep and somehow we both knew that tonight was the night, but how, where?? Neither of us could think of such a sin "in" the church building, the rectory next door was out of the question and her home was far too transparent with neighbors. Then the solution came to Evelina!

"My parents have a summer home on the river not too far from town. It is secluded and no one ever goes there unless it is a planned family outing. I truly think we would be safe there."

"Are you sure this is what you want", I asked. The smile on her face and the love in those eyes told me everything I needed to know. We both agreed to meet there within the hour.

Within the hour. The words resonated in my mind. Within the hour, I was going to finally experience what love truly felt like between a man and a woman. Within the hour, I was going to break my vows to God and the church, throw away eight years of college and seminary. Within the hour, my life would change forever.

Evelina arrived at the river home shortly before I pulled into the driveway. She had candles lit to give off enough light for us to move around and yet not attract attention in the unlikely event someone passed by. As I entered the cottage, her face was even more beautiful in the glow of candlelight. We fell together in a much awaited embrace. I gently kissed her for the first time and she kissed me back with a long, lingering kiss that will be forged into my mind until I die. We couldn't believe how much love we felt for each other and how much we wanted each other.

She looked up into my eyes, took my hand and led me to a bedroom.

Nervously, I began to undress her, feasting my eyes on the sheer perfection of her body. She helped me out of my clothes, hesitating slightly when it came to my collar. We stood naked in front of the candles on the nightstand, lost in the sensation of body against body, drinking in the smell and taste of skin. Unable to restrain ourselves any longer, we sank into the bed for our first taste of what God designed solely for a man and a woman in love - - - oneness.

As the hours passed, we devoured each other in love and lust. I ravished every inch of her body and was pleased to see how her body responded to mine. We knew what we were doing was wrong, but we were in love. We also knew we had to get back to our homes before anyone became suspicious.

As we laid there in each other arms she said "I wish we could just lie here and watch the sun come up".

I kissed her on the forehead for we both knew that was total folly. We dressed hastily and put the bedroom back like we found it, careful not to leave a clue of our rendezvous. After a long lingering kiss goodbye on the porch, we promised to meet whenever we could both get away.

Evelina left first in her fancy green 1917 Peerless Model 56 while I was fortunate to be driving a well-used 1911 Ford Model T provided by the church. I was happy not to be driving a horse and buggy as I did when I came to Rosenberg two years ago. So much had happened since I came to this town and now a major crisis, dilemma or a heaven sent opportunity. Whatever it was called, it was real and I had to deal with it. It all boiled down to one thought at that moment: we were in love and wanted to spend the rest of our lives together.

Chapter 7

TURNING POINT

I awoke the next morning foggy with the realization of what I had done. I found myself almost paralyzed with the fear that her parents, the Bishop and the parishioners would find out, not to mention my parents. Sin was the free and deliberate act that destroys or weakens our relationship with God and the proper relationship we should have with others. As I walked from the rectory to the church, I was ashamed, knowing that all sin is freely done. But when I entered the social hall at the church I saw Evelina's smile and all my fears and guilt melted away. Seeing her face told me that somehow we would work this out and somehow we would be together. When I am with Evelina, I want nothing more than to be a man.

We met several more times at the river house during the summer and fall. It seemed to be the only safe place where we could be away from prying eyes. The summer months were the times that we had to be extremely cautious. More of the town's folks visited their homes at the river and an occasional fisherman happened along. I wrestled with the Devil constantly knowing that ending our relationship was the right thing to do, but happiness like this was new to me and I wasn't willing to let it slip away. Despite the risks, each time we met was as loving and precious as the last and our love for each other simply grew stronger. We spoke of how to tell our parents and the Catholic Church, but each time we ended up tangled in strewn clothes and blankets from the bed. Swept away on a tidal wave of passion, we reveled in the bliss of our bodies, intertwined in peace and love. We always promised to have a meaningful conversation <u>the next time</u>, but the touch of her body, the smell of her hair was intoxicating, exhilarating, almost addictive. Addictive to the point that I knew without a trace of uncertainty that being her husband was the only thing that mattered in my life. Was I wrong to love her more than God? Was I forfeiting my very soul just for the privilege of loving a woman? Surely God would be merciful. Above being a Priest, I was a man, not an infallible being.

We both longed for a normal relationship where we could take long walks and tell each other our hopes, dreams and little secrets. The simple act of holding hands in public would have been a treasured experience, but for now stolen moments were all we could hope for. Our biggest challenge was to act normal at church and around others. We couldn't risk lingering glances, a brush of a hand or even the slightest sign of extra attention. Our lives had to go on as usual when we weren't at the river house.

Then one cold December night 1917 when we thought everyone was either at choir practice or busy with Christmas preparation, we got caught. Evelina's father came to the river house to hide a Christmas gift, a new bicycle, for her little brother. He had us "dead to rights" as he saw both of our cars in the driveway and our half-dressed bodies through the window. He kicked the door open, simultaneously screaming with rage and crying with disappointment. We did our best to explain, but her father was not a man to be reasoned with. His reputation as a shrewd businessman and town leader made him a force unto himself. He didn't want to hear that I was going to give up the

Priesthood or that we planned to marry. All he could think about was the shame and ridicule facing his family and the church. As afraid of him as I was at that moment, the images of my Mother's face and tongue-lashing in pure Czech was more terrifying. What a mess! What a predicament I have put Evelina and myself in! But then I turned and looked into her tearful eyes and knew that whatever the consequences, it would be worth it. A life with her was worth any amount of anguish. I knew then that the best in life is obtained only at the cost of great sacrifice.

Chapter 8

THE RECKONING

We tried unsuccessfully to reason with her father while we were scrambling to dress in front of him. Knowing it was a futile effort, we grabbed hands and ran to our cars. Leaving him there to stew in his anger seemed like the best plan of escape at the moment. I put Evelina in my car and drove her home. She was so distraught that I was afraid to let her drive and we needed these few moments to devise a plan.

"Let's go to my mother and explain everything before my father has a chance to give her the negative side of our situation. Perhaps she can calm him down, make him see that despite everything else, we were just two young people in love".

I agreed with her plan because I certainly didn't have any immediate family help to draw upon.

When we walked in the front door, Evelina's mother detected the terror on our faces but simply smiled and took our hands.

She said, "I have suspected this for a long time and knew that you both needed time to sort it out".

We took our first relaxed breath since her father stormed into the cottage.

"I plan to leave the Priesthood and marry Evelina. I am an educated man, I can provide a good life for your daughter and I promise you that I will love her always".

Her Mother said "I will try my best to reason with my husband and act as an intermediary with the church, but right now, you should go to the rectory and young-lady, you should retreat to your room, for your own sake!" We took our new allies advice and did just as she said.

When I entered the rectory I felt as alone and confused as I had ever been. The uncertainty of my impending punishment from the church and my mother struck terror into my soul. But they were not the owners of my soul - - - God was. God was my first priority, with Him I must make all this right. I fell to my knees, then flat on my face begging for forgiveness and understanding. I was seeking a harbinger of peace so I prayed for what seemed like hours until I must have fallen asleep. I awoke before dawn with the realization that God was a forgiving God. He knew me better than I knew myself and probably knew this would happen eventually. He knew I was forced into the Priesthood and He knew my weaknesses. He was undoubtedly disappointed in me, but I knew that He would forgive me.

The church and Evelina's Father were not so forgiving. I was summoned to the church conference room at 11:00 AM to find him, the Bishop and other church elders. All were sitting stately in their chairs with looks of disgust and condemnation. I had nothing to say except that I was sorry and I planned to marry Evelina. The rest was up to them. I sat silently while each one espoused his opinion and recommendation for resolution of the disgraceful situation we all found ourselves in. I sat erect, head up and took it like a man. Christmas was only 2 weeks away, which added to the church's dilemma. I was asked to leave the room after 2 hours of their relentless snipping, feeling as though I had been eviscerated. I told myself that I deserved every bit of their wrath but having Evelina for my wife as the end result made it all worthwhile. I went back to my office and waited for their verdict.

Another hour passed before the Bishop and Evelina's Father entered without knocking. Their final decision was for me to continue my Priestly duties through the Christmas season and into January. They felt this would be best for an unsuspecting congregation and would give the Diocese time to bring in a replacement. This whole debacle would be kept **absolutely quiet** as the result of a sworn oath amongst every person in that conference room. The Bishop would compose a letter to my parents to be sent yet this day. I agreed to their recommendations figuring these few weeks would give me time to make future plans for Evelina and me. We never had time to discuss where we would like to live or how many children we would have. The brevity of our visits never allowed time for such heartfelt discussions planning for our life together. They left my office and I went on with my day as if life was somehow "normal".

The only part of my Priestly duties that I dreaded was hearing confessions and dolling out penitence before granting absolution. I now felt unworthy to free others from their sins when I could not absolve myself of my transgressions.

Sunday Mass brought a flood of emotions. I felt blessed to be giving my services as their Priest. At the same time, I felt sick to my stomach wondering if they knew as I shook each hand after mass. Most of all I felt empty when I looked out over the congregation and didn't see Evelina with her family. I promised myself that I would visit her home after all the services this Sabbath.

As I approached her house, a sickening feeling came over me. I remembered that I did not see anger on her Father's face, only the look of a conqueror, or a cat looking at a mouse knowing it is trapped and helpless. Why wasn't Evelina in church this morning, she never missed a Sunday except when she was so ill. As I knocked and waited for her parents to open the door, a terrifying thought came over me.

When the door opened he was standing there with a "Holier-than-Thou" look on his face. He said, "I have been waiting for you Father Hajek. I wanted to be the one to tell you that **you** will never see Evelina again. I have sent her far away and you will **never** find her." My heart sank, my head spinning and my eyes filled with tears. **"Soon this town will be rid of you and this secret will die here**. So don't ever darken my door again and don't try to find her. I used all my resources to make sure that there is no trail for you to follow. She will start a new life and will soon forget that she ever knew you."

I looked past him and caught a glimpse of her Mother. I called out to her, begged her to help me, to help us, but to no avail. She was crying and had a look of utter defeat about her. Being his wife couldn't have been easy all these years. He slammed the door in my face. I was utterly defeated and heart broken. I felt the blood drain from my head; I felt the trembling of my hands and knees.   I could barely force my body to turn and walk down the porch steps and back to my car. How could this be happening? Two people in love should have the right to live a life together, to make their own choices. What right do these supposedly Christian people have to alter my life, my destiny?

The drive back to the rectory seemed endless. Now what would I do with my life? I wasn't going to be a Priest, a husband or a father to our children. An overwhelming feeling of doom came over me as I entered the rectory. I fixed myself a cup of coffee and sat in the parlor for hours trying to make sense of this whole mess. I was unable to convince myself that our love wasn't to be, because none of this made any sense. I knew that I wasn't the perfect Priest. That somehow Evelina filled a special spot in my heart that even God couldn't fill. If I were a perfect Priest, I wouldn't feel the need to fill that vessel with anything but God. I finally dragged myself up to bed in the wee hours of the morning hoping to catch a few hours of sleep.

The next few days were a blur to me. I got through by trying to act cheerful to the parishioners, especially the children this holiday season. However, the loneliness in my heart was almost more than I could bear. I had no one to talk to, no solace obtainable. Then just when I thought things couldn't get any worse, a letter from my parents arrived. I sat down at the table of my sparsely equipped kitchen before opening it. I didn't expect to find redemption on those pages, but I never expected to find myself exiled.

Chapter 9

DISOWNED

The letter was blunt and to the point. It was in English, but I knew that my Mother dictated every word. It read:

Edward,

Words cannot express how your actions have disgraced our family and the church. Your brother, Joseph, who just returned from the war, will be arriving in Rosenberg on January 15. He will bring along your few personal belongings. He will then drive you to Fort Worth, where you will board an east bound train to Nashville, Tennessee.

You have a fine education so you should be able to forge a life for yourself.

May God forgive you for your sins, for we will **not**.

Mother & Dad

MATKA & OTEC (in Czech)

I read that letter four times; the first time in shock, the second in disgrace, the third in heartbreak and the fourth in anger. Once again people were taking control of my life!!!! I am a 27 year old man and should have some say in my destiny. I wanted to rebel and fight back, but what good would that do. My church didn't want me, my family didn't want me and the only person I ever truly loved was sent far away. *Maybe going east was a good plan.* I could start over; put these past thirteen years behind me. The only thing I would take from Texas was my everlasting broken heart. That I would carry with me no matter where I lived. The memories and name Evelina will hold a special place in my heart until I go to my grave. I need no reminder of her, I carry her within me.

January 15 came quickly. The new Priest, turned out to be Father Ignatius J. Valenta, one of the men ordained the same day as I. It pleased me that my parish would be turned over to someone that I had known for years. He arrived a week early so I introduced him to the congregation, the rectory, and Rosenberg. I assured him he would have his hands full with this congregation as there were now 50 Catholic families in Rosenberg. He asked me why I was giving up my post in Rosenberg, although he was thrilled to have a permanent assignment. I merely told him I had other interest back east that had to be dealt with immediately.

My last mass was a bittersweet experience. The new Priest was brimming with enthusiasm and eager to take over the pulpit. I administered the Holy Sacraments for the last time, said good bye to the families I had come to know so well over the past 2 years. I also resigned my position as School Superintendent and said a tearful goodbye to the teachers and students with whom I had closely bonded.

Knowing I would never be returning to Rosenberg compelled me to drive out to the river house one last time. Tears filled my eyes as I approached the place where Evelina and I found such happiness. I didn't get out of the car, I couldn't move my legs. My body heaved as I sobbed looking at the house that brought such joy and now such a hollow feeling. I could feel her in my arms, see her smiling face and taste the pleasure of her body. I wasn't just going to miss her perfect body; I would miss the sheer joy of just being with her. These were all memories now, just sweet memories.

The saddest thing was realizing that I never even had the opportunity to say goodbye. It would have been the hardest thing I ever had to do, but it would have brought some sense of closure. Maybe we both could have come to realize that ours was a love unobtainable, forbidden by our parents and God.

Back at the rectory, I packed the last of my belongings and was ready for Joseph to arrive in the morning. I racked my brain for days trying to find a way to track Evelina, but he was right, there was no trail. I couldn't ask questions around town without raising suspicion, so I played along with the rest of the town who believed what they were told. "She went away to pursue an excellent educational opportunity". I wondered if Evelina would try to find me, if her love for me would over-power the fear of her father. But how would she find me? My mother was as ruthless as her father. She would never think of looking for me in Nashville. I wonder if she cried for me at night, as I did for her.

Joseph arrived at the rectory early the next morning. It was so good to see him and lock ourselves in a brotherly hug. I was so grateful that he made it back from the war unscathed. Even though he was four years my junior, he was wise beyond his years. He simply said, "Grab your things, Brother, and let me get you out of here".

The long 270 mile trip to Fort Worth in Joe's 1915 Model-T gave us plenty of time to catch up on the news from West. Eventually we got around to my problems.

Joseph started by saying "I feel for you, Edward, I truly do. I have always felt sorry for you, sorry that you were forced into becoming a Priest and was damn glad it wasn't me. We Hajeks are proud people and entrepreneurs. The thought of you getting cuts of meats from parishioners when they butchered instead of a decent salary just made me sick. Custom or no custom that is not your style. So tell me about the girl."

For the first time in weeks I felt a sense of relief come over me. It was a calmness, a sense of peace. At last I had someone to talk to. Joseph just married Harriet Sykora last year so he was eager to talk about love. He wanted to hear about my romance, and maybe even pick up a few tips about love making from his older brother. It was great to share some wholesome guy talk, brother to brother.

I started at the beginning and told him the whole story, only leaving out the most intimate details that will stay forever between Evelina and me. The trip went faster than we expected because of the lively conversation. It was so good to talk to my brother, bare my soul to him and receive his understanding. At that moment I felt like he was the Priest and I was confessing, seeking absolution.

He was told not to stop at West on the way to Fort Worth even though we went right by the town. I took one last look at the town I called home for fourteen years as we drove north.

I asked Joseph, "Was it both of our parents that disowned me or was it just our Mother"?

He replied with tears in his eyes, "It is mostly Mother. You know what a fanatic she is about religion. Dad went along with her demands, like he always has, just to keep peace. He told me that he has to live the rest of his life with her and he knew that you would find a way to come back to West."

The rest of the trip we talked about farming, politics, weather, and his involvement in the bloody war. Joseph asked, "What are you planning to do when you get to Nashville"?

I looked at him with a smirk on my face and said, "I will know the answer to that question only after I get to Nashville. I wonder why they picked Nashville of all places".

With that we turned into the train station, parked the car and gathered my bags. He handed me a one way ticket which was the final stake in my heart. We hugged goodbye, shook hands and took a long look into each other's eyes. The thought of possibly never seeing my little brother again cut deeply. I turned and walked toward my future - - - whatever that may be.

Chapter 10

EAST BOUND NASHVILLE, TENN.

1918

I boarded the train and got myself situated for the trip. Almost 700 miles on a train would prove to be a time for reflection and transformation. People were very polite to me, the 27 year old Priest. Mixed emotions caused me to swallow hard as the train pulled out of the station. I never planned to leave my beloved Texas, home of my ancestors, home of my future, but here I was, Eastbound. I told myself that Texas is not just a place on a map, but a place in my heart; therefore I would be taking Texas with me.

The miles slipped by, one by one, and I was intrigued by the vastness of Texas, most of which I had never seen. I spent hours simply staring out the window, contemplating my future. I looked to the sky hoping to find redemption looking me in the eye, so I prayed for forgiveness and help finding my new life.

We eventually crossed the state line into Arkansas, followed by a corner of Mississippi and finally Tennessee.

My heartbreak soon turned to thoughts of new beginnings. I had no idea how big this country was. I was dumbstruck to see the towns roll by and thousands of people living a totally different kind of lifestyle than how I was raised. There were endless possibilities for a young man willing to work at carving a future for himself. It was at that moment when I took off my collar. Seminarians referred to it as "the dog collar", a symbol of obedience. I boarded this train a Priest but I'm going to get off a free man. For the first time in my life, my destiny is completely in my hands. God gave me many talents and I plan to put them all to use. My trusty Prayer Book will be the only evidence of my Priesthood that I shall keep.

As soon as the train arrived in Nashville, I found a men's clothing store and bought some "civilian" clothes with the money I earned as School Superintendent. I changed into my new look in the fitting room and left my priest robe draped over the chair. I would like to have seen the look on the next guys face when he found the garb of the vanishing priest.

The size of Nashville was a bit overwhelming compared to Rosenberg. I found a cheap boarding house to live until I could find a job. My first order of business was to learn about Nashville and determine if we were a match. Why did my parents select Nashville, anyway? After all, I don't have to stay here. However, any future train tickets would have to come out of my meager funds.

Edward's New Look

Priests' were paid next to nothing and my boyhood farming days surely didn't net any money. Finding a job was paramount on my list of survival skills.

Reading the local papers and taking a tour of the town helped me to become familiar with what Nashville had to offer *a man starting from scratch*.

Nashville, Tennessee, circa 1918

Nashville, Tennessee, circa 1920

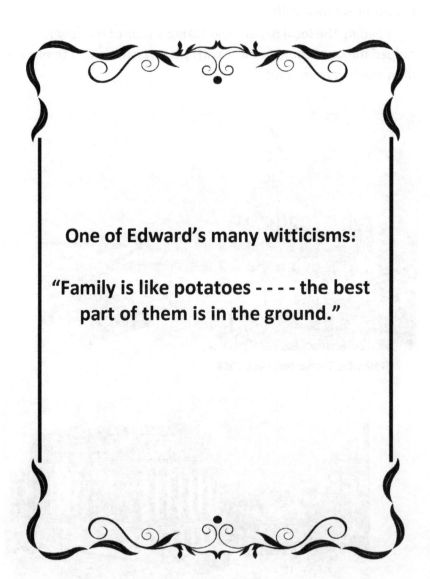

One of Edward's many witticisms:

"Family is like potatoes - - - - the best part of them is in the ground."

Chapter 11

REINVENTING MYSELF

The first thing that caught my eye was Vanderbilt University. I knew I loved to teach and that seemed like a natural fit. Preparing a resume' would be tricky. Hopefully explaining why I left the Priesthood could be skimmed over, while focusing on my superb eight year education, speaking four languages and teaching experience.

I struck out for Vanderbilt with my new suit, vest, tie, a business haircut and a formidable resume'. The hiring manager must have been distantly related to my Mother. His probing questions and dubious nature made my first interview somewhat intimidating. He informed me they had no need for a Czech teacher and all other positions were currently filled by qualified instructors. He would be happy to keep my resume' on file in the event an opening should become available. I tried hard not to show my disappointment and thanked him for his time.

As I was retreating to his office door, he said, "I am fascinated by your unique handwriting. Do you by any chance know calligraphy? I told him that I did indeed know calligraphy and would be happy to show him a sample of my work. Pleased with what he saw, he offered me a job teaching a class which just became open due to an unexpected illness. We agreed upon a salary and I would be starting tomorrow. Leaving his office I was simultaneously filled with pride and rejection. Teaching calligraphy was not what I had planned for the rest of my life, but it would provide food and shelter.

After a few months, the calligraphy class was going well, but I was not satisfied. I saw an advertisement for the Blackstone College of Law. Law school by correspondence has been in existence in the USA since 1890 when two schools merged and became the Blackstone College of Law. It was a well-respected college that graduated attorneys by "Reading the Law", as it was called back in those days, thus widely

Edward Teaching at Vanderbilt University, 1918

accepted. After further investigation I decided it was a good fit for me and I sent for the enrollment forms. I had enough money saved by this time to cover the tuition and books.

My meager room at the boarding house was the perfect retreat for me to study. My daily routine was becoming monotonous, had it not been for my studies. Early to rise, breakfast, off to Vanderbilt to teach, home, dinner and then study late into the night. At meal time I always gave the Blessing before we boarders shared a meal. On my first day there the proprietor asked if someone would be willing to give thanks for the food she so diligently prepared over a hot stove. No one offered so I instinctively told her I would be honored. It became part of each meal and I could see the questions on each face as they raised their heads. I didn't make my prayer of thanks too elaborate, but they were far better that what any of the others could have mustered up. They were probably asking themselves, "Who is this man"?

I was eager for a new challenge and found myself devouring the course material every evening and all week-end. At this rate I was on an accelerated path to become a lawyer, an occupation that I could take to any state in the Union once I passed their State Bar exam. Testing had never been difficult for me, so my confidence grew. It took me well over a year to complete all 30 volumes and pass all associated testing.

I was now ready to take the State Bar exams. I decided to "sit for the exams" in Tennessee, Alabama and North Carolina. They were adjoining states and opportunities may arise there. My testing skills came thru again and I was now a licensed Attorney in three states. Calligraphy might have saved me, but my love for education will provide a good living.

Chapter 12

HOMESICK

1919

It is now 1919 and up to this point I haven't had much time to think about Texas and what I left behind. An occasional letter from my brother kept me mildly informed of the happenings around West and our family. But not a day went by that I hadn't thought about Evelina. Wondering where she was, whether she married and had children by now nearly drove me crazy. The thought of another man holding her made me ache all over. Her father hid her well, for my brother kept his eyes and ears open for whispers or clues. Thus far the town merely thought she went away for more schooling. I assumed her Fathers' plan included her meeting someone else, getting married and starting a family. When the time was right he would bring her back to Rosenberg and integrate her back into the community. No one would be the wiser and she would never dare speak a word of the truth shaming his family and his church.

I laid in bed at night thinking about her and wondering what our life would have been like under different circumstances. We would have courted properly, had one of those festive Czech weddings and started a family by now. I longed to hold her and make love to her tenderly, almost being able to feel her soft skin and warm body against me. Then when the pain became too intense, reality would set in. I rolled over with tear filled eyes and tried to fall asleep, another lonely night in Nashville.

The morning light would come streaming through my easterly room at the boarding house. As I dressed for my Vanderbilt job, I dreaded another breakfast in the dining room with the revolving guests that have come and gone over the past two years. Rarely did I encounter someone with whom I could have an intelligent conversation. I was also becoming restless with the calligraphy class and the looks other professors gave me in staff meetings. In their minds, teaching calligraphy was well beneath them. Little did they know that I was now an attorney in three states and about to move on to the next chapter in my life.

Chapter 13

HANGING MY SHINGLE NORTH CAROLINA

1920

I applied to several law firms in Tennessee and a few in North Carolina. I interviewed with my top three choices and felt I had a pretty good chance of being employed with two of them. My decision was almost made when a letter arrived from a law firm in North Carolina expressing sincere interest in what I had to offer. I was not your typical 22 year old college graduate. I would soon turn 30, had eight years of college, a licensed attorney in three states and spoke four languages. This firm was a progressive establishment that planned to be of assistance to the thousands of immigrants arriving in America yearly. Eager to see what they had to offer, I made the trip to North Carolina.

The interview went well; their offer was more than I could have dreamed of as a novice lawyer. They wanted me to start in a month, which would make it January 3, 1920. Thrilled with my new challenge, I returned to Nashville and gave my notice to both Vanderbilt and the boarding house.

With the Christmas holiday and mid-term break, the month flew by before I knew it. I packed my few belongings and boarded a train headed east once again. I planned to arrive early enough to permit me ample time to look over the town and find living arrangements. My new salary at least permitted me to find more suitable housing. Gone was the three story clap-board, wrap around porch boarding house and eating meals with strangers. I found a nice apartment in a better neighborhood; however it was not extravagant by any means. My conservative upbringing taught me to only have what you need and save, save, save for the future. Who knows, maybe my future would finally allow me to think about dating and finding a wife. If I could only learn Evelina's status, I would either be on a train to retrieve her or be forced to move on. I was now in the position to offer her a decent standard of living.

I wrote to my brother, Joseph, out of sheer desperation. I felt like I had come to a crossroads in my life and I needed to know once and for all whether Evelina was going to be part of what lie ahead. I told Joseph about my new career in North Carolina and begged him to find something out, no matter what rock he had to overturn. Joseph was young and happily married therefore he understood what I was feeling and what I was missing in my life all these years.

Three weeks later I received a letter from him that would cause me to drop to my knees and weep.

Chapter 14

REVELATION

His letter told me how he made the trip to Rosenberg on the premise of a business meeting. Only brotherly love would make him lie to his loving wife. Once in Rosenberg he made subtle inquiries around town until he stumbled onto one of her school classmates working at the bakery. Over a steaming cup of coffee, she happily supplied him with bits of town gossip, which she thought was just idle curiosity. I asked her if there was a young lady named Evelina living in Rosenberg and instantly her gossip mode went into high gear.

"Oh yes, Evelina was just home for Christmas for the first time since her departure late in 1917. Do you know her"?

"No, a friend of mine knew her and mentions her name once in a while".

"Well, she's as beautiful as ever and seemed to be quite happy with her new family. Tell your friend that she's married, had a little girl not quite two years old and a baby boy less than three months old".

This fountain of information was flowing as fast as the coffee, as she topped off his cup.

"Evelina's family was telling everyone that the two year old was just big for her age, but Evelina confided in a girlfriend that she was pregnant when her father took her from Rosenberg. She didn't know that she was pregnant until after her speedy departure. She never told the girlfriend who the father actually was".

Lucky for Joseph, the girlfriend who couldn't resist telling the juicy gossip happened to be friends with the bakery employee.

As if all that news wasn't painful enough, Joseph went on to tell me in his letter of his suspicions that the little girl was mine. How could she just go on with her life as if our love never happened? How could she keep our child from me? Surely she knew that I would find her eventually. The pain of never having her and our daughter nearly killed me until one day I came to realize that her diabolical father must have threatened her with something horrible. In my heart of hearts, I knew that she pined for me the same way I yearned for her. So whatever he threatened her with must have had a degree of finality to it.

Over the next 6 months I tried to come to grips with her decision. Going back home to claim her and our daughter as mine would only serve one purpose - - my ego. I realized that I must once and for all accept our new lives and begin my own quest for love and happiness. I had only experienced happiness as a boy on the farm in West and in the arms of Evelina in Rosenberg. The other half of my life has been a struggle and heart-breaking to say the least.

Czechs are a strong, proud people and I was more determined than ever to make myself, and hopefully my family proud. Maybe someday I could go back to West and hold my head high.

Chapter 15

NEW BEGINNINGS

When I interviewed for the attorneys position in North Carolina I made a solemn vow. I told myself if I took that position, I was going to change everything about my shattered past. I even changed the pronunciation of my last name. I introduced myself as Edward Hajek (pronounced Hike) in contrast to the proper pronunciation of Hajek (pronounced Hyak). I was prepared to make a fresh start with no ties to West, Rosenberg or Texas.

January 3 came quickly and I was eager to use my new skills and help people with their legal issues. I was given a mid-size office, without a view, but I was quite pleased. After all, I never practiced law before and was grateful for the opportunity afforded to me with this job.

The weeks and months flew by and the complexity of cases given to me increased expediently. I enjoyed working with the clients and the research required to have a successful outcome on each case. I was with the firm almost a year when a new partner took over and changed the whole operandi of the firms original philosophy. His sole reason to be a successful law firm was to make money - - and lots of it. No longer were we concerned with the wellbeing of the clients who were mostly struggling immigrants. Now we were racking up billable hours and dragging out cases that could have been settled out of court.

It appeared that things were not going to change back to the beliefs for which I signed on originally. Therefore, I told myself it was time to look for employment elsewhere. I had become so disillusioned with the inner-workings of a law firm that I began exploring the possibility of opening my own law office. Life has taught me to be a loner, so maybe I could make it on my own as an ethical attorney. I visited some towns in need of a law office and found Richmond, Virginia to be my best prospect. I immediately began studying for the Virginia Bar exam. I passed their Bar exam with ease and was now licensed in 4 states. Giving that notorious partner my resignation was one of the highlights of my life.

Chapter 16

RICHMOND, VIRGINIA

1921

I now have both the education and the confidence to be successful. I packed up and moved to Richmond not realizing that my life would take another dramatic turn in the near future. I found a suitable apartment not far from the downtown area, figuring that the bustling city would present more opportunity for clients. Within days I found a small office for rent that looked professional yet austere.

My new office was just one block from the city square, offered on street parking, as automobiles were becoming more in vogue. I would have my name painted on the half glass door in bold black letters, edged with gold. EDWARD J. HAJEK - - - - - - ATTORNEY AT LAW. As you entered there was a small open office suitable for a secretary/receptionist. For now I would just tell my clients that she was out to lunch or off for the day. Straight ahead was a solid wooden door which opened into my office. It had a sizeable desk, 4 file cabinets and a wall of bookshelves which would house my growing collection of law books, reference material and journals. Oh yes, and the Bible. I hadn't been going to church much since I've been on my own. I think I partially blamed God for my plight. I laid in bed at night sometimes and wonder who really was to blame; God, my Mother, Evelina's Father or myself. Then to clear my mind for sleep, I would pray earnestly still asking for forgiveness and now asking for guidance in this new chapter of my life. Down deep I was still a Priest and a devout Catholic.

I was open for business within a week. I had the office painted before I moved in and placed an advertisement in the local newspaper which would run twice a week for several months. Next I joined a couple of the local service clubs and introduce myself to other businessmen. Business was a little slow in the beginning, so I applied for a teaching position at the Massey Business College, at 300 W. Grace Street. I started out teaching English classes and then was asked to teach a pre-law course. Finally word of my law services weaved its way into the conversations at dinner parties and country club golf outings. Business picked up to the point where I hired a legal secretary and we kept busy meeting court deadlines and appointments. I convinced the Dean of the college to switch my law classes to the evenings so I could do both jobs well.

Once again I found myself too busy to think about women or family life. But fate has a way of taking charge. I was invited to a friend's house for a Christmas gathering. It was a rather large affair with his family and friends all home for the holidays. I purchased an appropriate hostess gift and presented myself at their festively decorated front door and rang the doorbell. When the door opened there stood the most beautiful woman that I had ever seen, since Evelina.

She said "Hello, welcome, my name is Hettie. I am an old friend of the family and who are you?"

I was so struck by her beauty, bubbly manner and her confidence that I could barely form words to answer her question. Finally I said, "And hello to you. I'm Edward Hajek, I also am a friend of the family."

She took my coat and hat and sat the gift on a table. Before I knew what hit me, she slipped her arm through mine and waltzed me into the parlor and began to introduce me to the guests with whom I was not acquainted.

After a while she was summoned to the kitchen and I found my host. We exchanged pleasantries, after which I blurted out, "who is Hettie and why haven't I seen her before"?

Chapter 17

NEW ROMANCE

Hettie and I spent the rest of the evening talking and getting to know each other. I haven't felt a flutter in my heart like this since I left Texas, since that last night with Evelina.

"I know you are an attorney here in Richmond".

"Well since you know all that, I should know more about you, Miss Hettie".

"I am a secretary for the Chesapeake and Ohio Railroad Co. here in Richmond. My home is a small town right across the state line in Stem, North Carolina. My parents own a small tobacco farm and I'm thrilled to be working in the city. I love the south and its traditions, but farming is not for me".

Hettie Hicks Overby, 1921

It was obvious that she was too much of a lady to enjoy working with chickens and mules. I told her about my farming days in Texas, my college education, my love for teaching and the law, but never once uttered the words - - Priest or seminary. That was part of my past and I would do everything in my power to keep it buried deep in my soul, never to be spoken of again. Of course, the question of why I pronounced my name "Hike" and not "Hyak" like others do came up eventually. I simply told her that is how my family pronounces it and ended the inquisition abruptly.

The party was over far too soon and I found myself standing at the front door, coat and hat in hand, saying goodbye to everyone, thanking the host and hostess for a lovely evening. Hettie stood by the door with the glow of the Christmas tree outlining her smiling face. I smiled and politely told her how fortuitous that we were both invited to the same party. We had both talked earlier in the evening that it was the "classic set-up", for which we were both grateful. I nodded my head towards the porch and she picked up on the cue instantly. She followed me outside, slipping that arm through my arm again. My knees melted.

Knowing that we only had a few moments, I got right to the point. "Hettie, could I see you again"?

She replied, "Why yes, I thought you were going to leave without asking."

"May I take you to dinner Friday evening? I will pick you up after work".

"Of course, Edward, I would love that".

I squeezed her hand, and gave a final wave goodbye to everyone on the porch and those peeking out the window. I think they were pleased with the results of their "match-making".

I thought about Hettie all week long. Those eyes, that soft skin, her intoxicating smile. Pangs of guilt and thoughts of Evelina hit me a few times, but I told myself that she moved on and so should I. After all, she married and had two children. True one of them might be mine, but I was denied the opportunity to be her husband and father to our daughter. I must move on and make a normal life for myself. I turned 32 years old two days after Christmas and it is past time for me to marry and start a family.

Friday evening finally arrived and I was waiting outside her office building downtown, leaning against the railing, trying to look suave and handsome. It was a cold winters evening, but the stars were shining brightly in the sky. She bounced down the steps with a few co-workers, introduced me and we were off together. Little did we know that we would be "off together" for the rest of our lives. We dined at a nice restaurant, celebrating my birthday and soaking up the joy of simply being together.

We dated exclusively for the next four months. It was liberating to take my girlfriend out in public, do fun things that young people did and not be looking over my shoulder, guarding every thought and word. She loved to dance and insisted that we frequent establishments that not only offered good food, but also lively dancing. Telling her that I knew

Happy Times, 1922

103

nothing about dance didn't stop her.

She said, "Well, then it is high time you learned".

She would grab my hand and drag me onto the dance floor. After a few nights of stepping on her toes and missing her cues, this old farm boy surprised himself. The Charleston, the Black Bottom, the Peabody and the Turkey Trot were all the rage and we were good at it. I was actually cutting loose and having fun, something that eluded me up to this point. It really didn't matter what we were doing, we just enjoyed being in each-others company. In love and joyously happy we announced our engagement the end of April. Neither of us wanted a fancy wedding, a far cry from the Czech wedding traditions.

I sent an invitation to my family back in Texas hoping that the animosity would be over now that I was marrying and found my path in life.

I received a reply from my Father expressing his regrets and saying that my Mother would never forgive me for leaving the Priesthood.

My brother, Joseph, also sent his regrets, however he had a legitimate excuse. His wife had been ill and he was tied down with the family.

Marriage Certificate – May 20, 1922

Nevertheless, on May 22, 1922, I married Hettie Hicks Overby in a lovely garden ceremony with Hettie's family and a few friends. At last I was in love, I was happy and we were going to make a good life for ourselves.

Edward and Hettie Hajek – Wedding Day

I had saved enough money to put a sizable down payment on a home in Richmond. My law practice was thriving and I still taught some classes at the Massey Business College. Furnishing our new home was one of the happiest times of my life. Hettie told me what she picked out that day and I must take her to look at it before making a final decision. We were two love birds, feathering our nest. In March 1923, Hettie met me at the door after work with a different kind of smile on her sweet face.

"I have wonderful news Edward, you're going to be a Father"! I was so elated that I picked her up and swirled her around.

"Oh Hettie, I must not hurt you", as I gently placed her on the sofa. "We must tell your family and buy furniture for the nursery and select a name".

Then on October 22 our first daughter, Hettie Doris, was born. We were beaming with the pride and joy that all new parents experience.

In the midst of our joy, my brother, Joseph was experiencing deep sorrow. His wife passed away November 21, 1924 in West. Hettie insisted that I go home to console Joseph.

She said, "Doris and I will be fine. We're surrounded by nice neighbors and my family is not far away."

What she didn't realize is that I wasn't welcome in West. This will be the first time that I have gone back to visit since my departure January 1918, six long years ago. I was told to arrive after dark and park my car in the back or in a garage. I was pretty much going to be under house arrest during the entire visit. However, I needed to do this for Joseph. It broke my heart to see the look of desperation on Josephs' face having been left alone with a young daughter to raise. I tried to console him all the while wondering why our Mother wasn't there. Joseph finally told me she retreated to her bedroom upon my arrival in West. I left Joseph with a heartfelt prayer.

Despite my dysfunctional family, the next few years were filled with wonderful memories of my newly formed family. Coming home to Hettie and Doris brought me great joy. I even enjoyed visiting Hettie's home and her relatives. It had been so long since I was surrounded by loving family that I decided to forego all the "in-law" predispositions and just enjoy the gatherings. It was a bit disconcerting though to see Hettie's mother "take snuff with a twig from a beech tree". She would cut a twig from the tree, splinter the ends of it, dip it in the snuff and rub it inside her lower lip. Other than that habit, she was a lovely southern lady and gracious hostess. Watching them farm tobacco with their mules entertained both little Doris and me.

Overby Gathering – Stem, North Carolina
Hettie: Third Row, Center

Hettie on Family Tobacco Farm

Then on August 25, 1927, Jacqueline Patricia, our second daughter was born. Hettie wanted both the girls baptized in the Methodist Church and took them to church with her each Sunday. I went along occasionally, but found it more comfortable using work as an excuse to *not* find myself face to face with God. Most Sundays, I would drop them off at church and then I would go to the office to work. Often prayer would find its way into my head during those moments of quiet reflection. I guess old habits die hard.

Edward Holding Hettie Doris 1925

Sunday afternoons were family time. During the summer months we would take the girls to the park, make homemade ice cream and play games. I started to become interested in photography since I had 3 lovely subjects with which to work. It was just another interest for an ever present inquisitive mind.

Both of my careers, law and teaching, were doing well. Then one evening at the college, an associate approached me about an offer he learned of with a business school in Olean, New York. My associate and his family were not about to leave Virginia so he told me about what appeared to be an appealing opportunity.

I inquired with the Westbrook Academy, a business college in Olean. The deal was for a new partner to take over the school when the elderly owner retired. The salary, ownership potential and demographics all appeared promising. I approached Hettie

Edward Holding Jacqueline Patricia 1929

about moving north, knowing leaving the south would be an enormous sacrifice for her to make. Olean was located in western New York and snows off Lake Erie would be troublesome. It took her a couple of days to mull it over before she agreed to the move. She was willing to do whatever it took to keep her husband and family happy.

I reached an agreement with the school owner and began to make plans to uproot my life once more. However, this time a career move also affected my family.

Before we moved north to Olean, I had to make one more trip to Texas. Joseph's 8 year old daughter, Marjorie, died on April 10, 1929 in West. Even though he remarried November 25, 1925, the death of his first wife and now his daughter by her was devastating. I owed it to him to pay a visit and maybe even counsel him on his grief. I still had my

Joseph Emil and Jennie Lee Hajek Wedding Day - November 25, 1925

priestly training tucked deep inside of me. I took the train and got there two days after the funeral. He would want our Mother at the funeral and I couldn't risk her not attending because I was there. He picked me up at the train station and invited me to stay with him. We shared the best three days as brothers that we had since we were children on the farm.

Joseph's Daughter, Marjorie

109

We never left his house as I was still not well received in West. It was with great joy that I opened his front door one afternoon and saw my Father standing on the porch. It had been years since our eyes met and he hugged me like a grizzly. The sheer joy of father and son reuniting caused us both to cry. It meant everything to see him and have a long conversation. He told me that my Mother would be furious if she found out, but enough time had passed honoring her unreasonable wishes. He wasn't getting any younger and he wanted to be part of my life. I felt a little better about myself when I left West this time. Forgiveness is a sweet elixir.

Chapter 18

NORTH BOUND
OLEAN, NEW YORK

1929

Back home from Texas, it was now time to finalize our move to Olean. I closed down my law office, resigned from the Massey Business College, packed up our house and family, and headed north. My plan was to work side by side with the owner until he retired then buy the school. In addition, I practiced law out of the large home we bought. Upon entering the foyer, the room on the right had towering dark wooden columns. We agreed that room would be perfect for my law office. I put my photography studio upstairs, where I also developed, printed and enlarged pictures for customers. I became fond of photography and found it relaxing. I won several awards for photographs that I took around town and of the children. It was the beginning of The Great Depression and making a comfortable living for my family was paramount. I was glad that I had a steady stream of income from all three of my vocations.

Hettie and Doris were excited about buying winter clothes and decorating a new home. Jacqueline was only two so

Jacque and Dick outside Photography Studio – 1936

taking her "blank-ie" was her only concern. When we arrived in Olean the snows had not yet started to fall. Thank Heavens, or I think Hettie would have turned around and returned home. Olean was nothing like Richmond. The temperatures and the people were colder. Gone was the southern hospitality and sitting on the front porch on a lazy summer afternoon talking to folks as they walked down the street. We got busy unpacking and establishing a new life for our family. Doris would enter first grade this year and I needed to acquaint myself with my new partner at the school. I prayed that this would work out because teaching is what I truly enjoyed. There is something fulfilling about setting the paths of young people and watching them prosper in the community.

The next couple of months brought new challenges which were met head on by all of us. The foreboding winters were probably the biggest hurdle. It was so cold that snow began falling in October. The neighborhood children would build statues and furniture out of snow in October and they would still be there in early May. Hettie gave the children cod liver oil to supplement their vitamin D.

Now that my Father and I were on speaking terms, I found myself yearning for his counsel on things that had been shelved

Hajek Family – 1931
Edward, Hettie (pregnant with Richard),
Jacqueline, Doris

for so many years. Easter break from the school seemed like a good time to pay him a visit and introduce him to Doris who was a mature seven year old. She was excited about the train ride and meeting her cousins. When we arrived in Fort Worth, she was wearing a sky blue coat and hat, and playfully skipped across the railway tracks towards Joe and his daughter, Julie, now five. The girls had a grand time playing with their dolls and getting to know each other. As usual, we stayed at Joe's new home in Fort Worth and Father drove up from West to visit. A deep satisfaction swept over me as we sat on Joe's front porch for hours talking and catching up. I was fourteen when they sent me to St. Mary's Seminary and now he's getting to know me as a man, a family man.

Snow wasn't the only thing the cold in Olean produced. On November 13, 1931, Hettie gave birth to our son, Richard Joseph. He was an enormous baby, weighing in at 11 pounds, 13 ounces. Hettie was so exhausted and sick after the delivery that it was necessary to call for her niece, Helen, from North Carolina to come help out the family. Hettie took to her bed for almost a year and Helen stayed the entire time.

One day while lying in bed nursing Richard, she looked up at me with those kind eyes and said "Edward, it's a good thing you finally got the son you have always wanted because this is our last baby"!

I smiled at her and acknowledged her ultimatum. She knew me so well, for secretly I did want a son to carry on the Hajek name.

I tried to help out with the girls by walking them down to Foley's Drug Store for ice cream in the summer months. I became fast friends with Mr. Foley, the owner, as we loved to swap jokes and stories. He had a thriving business as everyone in Olean enjoyed getting out into the warm sunshine June thru August. In the winter, I bundled Dick up in his snow suit, prop him up on the sled with three sides and walk him and the girls to the park. There the girls joined in the sledding or ice skating

Edward and Richard - 1932

while I held my toddler son on my lap. As I sat there in the sheer joy of these precious moments, I thanked God for blessing me with three perfect children. I promised to be a good father and would never send one of my children away. No matter how old I became, I just could not shake that memory.

During the summer of 1934, we were all thrilled when my Father made the trip by himself to visit us. He was 66 years old, still standing proud and tall. Over the years he lost some of his Czech accent and a hint of that Texas drawl would slip out occasionally. Hettie and the children were fascinated by him and his stories of Texas and his heritage. I was so pleased that my family got to meet him and grow to love him as I did. He possessed a gentle soul and "not a ruffled bone in his body", as another Texas relative once said. He simply was a sweet, kind man. To hide his disappointment, Father told my family that my

Mother wasn't up to the trip and nobody thought to question him.

Joseph Victor's Visit from Texas, 1934

In the midst of my baby boom, I was running into problems at the business school. The owners' nephew began to work there and little by little I could see that HE would be the one taking over the school when retirement day arrived. After a couple of years, I decided it wasn't worth the fight because Hettie was becoming more and more disillusioned with New York and it's cold weather. After explaining all this to my Father during his visit, his advice was for me to head back south and find a permanent location to settle. I had moved my family around enough and they deserved stability.

By the fall of 1935 I found a position as Administrator and Teacher at the Norfolk College in Norfolk, Virginia. Hettie and the family were thrilled to be going back below the Mason-Dixon Line. Things went well there, but I still wanted to own my own business college someday. I needed to save some more money and find that permanent place my Father spoke of in his wise counsel.

Hajek Family, 1935

Norfolk was a congenial town, offering everything my family and I needed. But I was longing to see Texas again. In the summer of 1936, I conjured up the idea that my Mother would welcome her grandchildren with open arms and finally grant me the forgiveness that I so dearly longed for. Jacque was nine and Dick, five, both eager to take their first vacation to Texas and see their Grandfather again. I never invited Hettie on one of my visits for fear that she would pick-up on some tidbit of information casually inserted into family conversations. My Priesthood was the only thing I ever kept from her. What could her knowing possibly add to our relationship? I couldn't bear to see the look on her face when I told her about my first love, Evelina and the possibility of me having a daughter by her. Hettie wasn't much of a traveler and all the moving around we did as a family was enough to last her a lifetime. She was perfectly happy to stay home and keep the fires burning. Doris was thirteen and wanted no parts of travelling with her younger siblings. "She would stay home and take care of Mother", she proudly injected. Doris had a kind spirit and loved to do things for others.

It was a long drive to Texas and the children became restless and bored. We played words games, counted cows and did all the typical road trip adventures. Making this trip alone with two children was probably a mistake. However my biggest mistake was giving in to Dick's pleading for a rather large bag of candy while we were passing through Arkansas. Jacque was in the front seat with me and we never dreamed that he would try to eat the whole bag at one sitting. Eventually he was complaining of a stomach ache and shortly after that nature intervened. He proceeded to throw-up all over the inside of the car, causing an odor that lingered for several miles to come. No matter what I did to clean the car, it still had that retched smell of vomit. I also discovered that little girls learn the "I told you so" characteristic at a very young age. I could just hear Hettie's voice as Jacque rebuked my actions.

Anticipation coursed through my body as we finally arrived in West. I timed our arrival so it was a Sunday afternoon and I knew the family would be gathered for dinner at home after Mass and Father wouldn't be working at the furniture store. I parked my car around back per customary instructions and proudly bounced up the steps, eager to present my two youngest children. When the door opened, Father and Joseph were inviting us in. Inside I found Joseph's new family and no one else. I asked Father where Mother was, but he lowered his head and uttered one word that cut like a knife - - - - "no".

They offered us food and drinks and the conversation flowed. The nine cousins sat on the floor of the parlor with Jacque and Dick in the center. They asked questions and played games like children do after the getting acquainted jitters wear off. They told my children how Grandmother didn't speak English and her only interaction with them was drawing a circle on the palm of their hands, saying "good child" in broken English.

I had a great time telling jokes to Joe's children. They were polite and always laughed even though I don't think they understood all of them. I decided to stay at the hotel since Joe had seven children by this time. It saddened me that Mother didn't come see us. How could any woman NOT want to meet her grandchildren after all these years? What kind of hold did her religion have on her mind that would keep her from forgetting about the past. After all, Christ died to forgive us for our sins. Was she that much more of a martyr?

We had a nice visit, but after three days I decided to start the arduous journey home. Jacque and I promised each other not to let the candy episode play out again. As the miles past one by one, I was trying to come up with a plausible reason why my own Mother wasn't there to meet us. Hettie would probably see right through me, but I would make up some excuse. Back in Norfolk, Hettie and Doris met us with open arms, complete with a scrumptious dinner, as Doris was becoming quite a good cook for her young age. She spent hours in the kitchen with Hettie, eager to learn more culinary tricks. We took turns telling our stories, careful not to mention Dick's encounter with the candy monster. I know Hettie detected the sadness in my eyes when we talked about the Texas family. I think she has always known there was a tragic disconnect between me and my family, but was too kind to ask much about it.

We were all back to our daily routines after the vacation time ended. Work was going well but that nagging dream of school ownership still festered in me. One day I asked a book salesman from the Southwest Publishing Company, whom I respected immensely, to keep his eyes open for a place that could use a business college. He eventually reported back to me that Maryland was his choice. Cumberland was ripe for a school, but it was mountainous and isolated. Hagerstown was his first choice. He and I went to both towns and his assessment was accurate. I talked to town leaders and decided that Hagerstown is where we would put down our final roots.

Chapter 19

OUR LAST STOP HAGERSTOWN, MD

1938

Having made my decision to focus solely on a business college and stop practicing law came without regret. I decided that you couldn't have a conscience and be a lawyer. I always prided myself on being an honest, upstanding man and some of the tactics used by other attorneys forced me to stoop to their level a few times to win my case. Now at the age of 48, I must settle on one career path and teaching has always been my passion.

In 1938 we made our last move. It was to Hagerstown, Maryland, located below the Mason-Dixon Line, but barely. I loaded my family into our 1929 Essex car and made our last drive from Norfolk to Hagerstown. I had $3,000 in my pocket and a head full of dreams.

Hettie said, "What are we going to do if this school fails, Edward"?

**1929 Essex Car that Brought the Hajeks
to Hagerstown, Maryland**

I said, "My dear Hettie, failure is not an option".

Convinced that teaching was born in me, I was determined to start my own school. In the beginning, I would focus on secretarial and accounting classes. I rented office space in the Professional Arts Building on the square and was pleased I had twelve students my first year. Enrollment increased to 75 students the second year.

We rented half a double house at 521 Summit Avenue which was conveniently located to the Surrey Elementary School. City Park was just a block away and gave the children a marvelous place to play. The family was settling into Hagerstown quite well, it actually felt like home. The children took great pride in memorizing our phone number which was 1642R.

HOTEL ALEXANDER – HAGERSTOWN, MARYLAND

The trolley passed right in front of our house and for 10 cents you could ride to the town square. The trollies turned around in the square and would take Hettie and the children back home after shopping. I joined several service clubs and became active in community endeavors.

I chose Hagerstown because it was a growing hub for industry, agriculture, and education for Maryland, Pennsylvania, and West Virginia. The Maryland Panhandle, where Hagerstown was founded in 1762, is only eleven miles wide. Dating back to the American Revolution made it deeply steeped in history. Hagerstown experienced a 69% increase in population between 1910 and 1922.

By 1940, Hagerstown was home to 32,941 residents. I read in a 1923 journal, that "Hagerstown is a natural distributing center for the Shenandoah Valley and the Cumberland Valley. It has five railroads: the Philadelphia & Reading, Pennsylvania, Norfolk & Western, Western Maryland, and the Baltimore & Ohio."

This growing city was home to many mills and factories producing silk, flour, grain, hose, gloves, ribbon, shoes, chemicals, cement, furniture, and machinery. Hagerstown is also home to Moller, the world's largest pipe organ company. Outside the city limits were productive farms, dairies, and orchards.

All of these growing business indicators told me that Hagerstown was over-due for a top-notch business college.

One of my goals was to see that my children were properly educated. Without giving myself away regarding my elite education, I insisted that our family speak proper English. We made a game of learning a new word daily. The children were getting so good at the game that I would throw in a tricky word like "perspicacity": having or showing an ability to notice and understand things that are difficult or not obvious. I recommended good books to the children as reading assignments. English was the foundation to their learning and I wished only to pass down selective bits of my education, never offering to teach them Greek, Latin or any Theological Precepts. We often spoke of history and literature in the evenings before our first television appeared in 1948.

I aptly named the school "The Hagerstown Business College". Advertising and my recruitment visits to surrounding high schools paid off, as enrollment flourished. I now had almost 200 students and growing. My goal was to make it the premier business college in the region. My only competition was the Columbia Business College on Antietam Street, owned by Sylvester Funk. We became fierce competitors and I must admit

I was happy when he announced the closing of his school in later years.

Tensions in Europe had been brewing for years however, 1938 events sent a chill through every Czech-American immigrant. Germany, Italy, Great Britain and France signed the Munich agreement which forced the Czechoslovak Republic to cede the Sudetenland, including the key

Edward J. Hajek
Opening Hagerstown Business College - 1938

Czechoslovak military defense positions, to Nazi Germany. The Czech Texans feared for their relatives back in their homeland, but thanked God that they were now Americans. March 15, 1939, under German pressure, the Slovaks declare their independence and formed the Slovak Republic. The Germans occupied the rump Czech lands, which was in violation of the Munich agreement, thus forming a Protectorate of Bohemia and Moravia. I was feeling secure as an American and grateful that my grandfather had the foresight to come to this new land in 1854.

In 1940, I bought a summer home near Dam # 4 on the Potomac River in Williamsport, Maryland. I must admit that seeing the house sitting next to the river took me back to Rosenberg and the indelible memories of Evelina. I don't think of her as often as I did during all those early years of torment. Who knows, maybe I bought this house subconsciously thinking it would bring me happiness instead of the heartbreak in Rosenberg. Maybe I would sit on the front porch and feel her presence. I think I surprised my whole family when I decided to put a new roof on the river house. My farm upbringing taught me to fix almost anything, so how hard could a roof be? Doris's fiancée, Dave, was good with tools and his help came in handy. Besides, he was trying to impress his future father-in-law. I soon realized that I wasn't a young farm boy any longer and this would be my last attempt at a large scale project. Little did Dave and I know that he and Doris would spend their honeymoon here at the Dam # 4 house. At the time of their marriage, Dave was a 2nd Lieutenant in the Army Chemical Warfare Division. He was only able to obtain a short military furlough during wartime for his wedding and honeymoon.

August, 1942, I received word my Mother was very ill and told I should make the trip to West to see her. Not wanting to make the trip myself, I solicited the help of a friend and typewriter salesman, William Cochran, to help with the driving. I also thought it wise to take Dick along as he was 10 years old by now and could learn from the journey. Jacque also decided to make the trip in order to get to know her cousins better. We stayed at a hotel in Fort Worth, but I made the drive to West myself. I was determined to see my Mother for the first time in 25 years. Her stroke left her in no condition to be barking insults or giving orders as to whom she would see or not see. My Father agreed that it was probably going to be the last time I would ever see her. When I entered her bedroom, her body stiffened, but she never uttered a word. I sat with her for over an hour, telling her about my life and my family. It was probably my imagination, but I thought I saw a glimmer of acceptance in her eyes a few times, yet she spoke not a single word. How I was hoping she could speak to me or at least squeeze my hand once to reignite that bond between Mother and Son, but that didn't happen. It was my Fathers' wish to have a picture taken with their three children. We carried Mother outside, placed her in a chair and proudly posed for a truly "one of a kind" photograph of our splintered family. It was a cherished moment.

Only Picture of Entire Hajek Family – August 1942
Left to Right: Edward John, Joseph Emil, Mary
Seated: Joseph Victor and Juliana

Joe now had eight children with his new wife, Jennie. She was a graduate of Baylor University and a Baptist. My Mother was so outraged that Joe didn't marry a Catholic that Joe finally packed up his family and left West years ago. He moved to Fort Worth where he opened a thriving garage. Dick and Jacque enjoyed spending time with them and getting to know them better. He and his cousin Edward were a dirty mess when they came in one evening after trying to dig a tunnel and cave to play in. The girls took Jacque to the school and introduced her to their friends. Dick and Jacque both relayed stories from the cousins of how Grandmother would request to see all of them. She was bedridden for some time and the children were understandably afraid of her because she was such an angry woman. They would line up at her bedroom door and take turns going to her bedside where she would draw that infamous circle on their palms and say "good child". Each child would then bolt out of her room when she was finished.

The long drive home to Maryland gave me plenty of time to relive in my mind both childhood memories and adult disappointments. Mother passed away a few months later leaving me at peace with the knowledge that I made the trip back to be with her before she went to her Heavenly reward.

World War II was in full swing by 1942, and I could feel it taking its toll on enrollment. Young men were joining the military in record numbers leaving necessary jobs open for young women to fill their void. During the war enrollment dropped off to the point where we had to let the janitor go and my family cleaned the school which now occupied the entire fifth floor. I had to become creative to earn enough money to feed my family and keep the doors open at the school. I offered my services in translating Latin, Greek and Czech information that towns' people had regarding the war. And once again I called upon my calligraphy skills to bale me out of a tight spot. Hagerstown was home to a large aircraft manufacturing company called Fairchild. They were handing out Army/Navy E Certificates to top achievers and asked me to "pen" the recipients' name and other pertinent information. I would take my son, Dick, along to the school to help expedite the process. I would sit at the instructors desk to the front of the classroom, pen the inscriptions on the over-sized certificates and an eager ten year old would carefully put both arms under the certificates and ever so carefully, taking tiny steps, would place one certificate on top of each student desk to dry. One by one he would fill up each desk, isle by isle. We received 10 cents per certificate. The sheer volume of certificates requested is the only thing that made it financially feasible.

My involvement in the community helped to cement the excellent reputation that the college had achieved. I even played Santa for years for the Kiwanis Club. Every Christmas morning Dick and I loaded the car with gifts either purchased by or donated to the club. I climbed into the very authentic looking red suit, complete with pillows, and we drove down to Boonsboro to the San Mar Orphanage. It was exhilarating to see the looks of anticipation and the sheer joy on their faces. Dick never questioned why a fake Santa visited them, when the real Santa left gifts at his house last night. However, he did comment one time that the San Mar Santa, as he called me, was requiring fewer pillows for stuffing each year.

By 1945, World War II was finally winding down. This dreadful war claimed the lives of 420,000 US military. Only the death toll of the Civil War at nearly 500,000 Union and Confederate lives would surpass the human cost of this war. Battle weary men, feeling lucky to be alive, were at last coming home to their families. They rightfully began to reclaim their old jobs which were so gallantly filled by young women during the past four years. These ladies were now interested in obtaining an advanced education in secretarial and nursing jobs, having had their fill of factory work. We obtained a contract with the government under the GI Bill to provide education to its returning veterans. I found it necessary to hire additional teachers to keep up with the demand as enrollment spiked. I started looking for property to buy as expansion was imminent. I also needed to find a larger house for my family. We soon moved to Funkstown, just a couple of miles from Hagerstown. It had larger rooms enabling the family to spread out a little more. Now that the children are almost grown, they seem to require more room to keep peace in the household. It had a much larger yard, but that would be Dick's responsibility. He's fourteen years old and I think back to what I was asked to do as a lad on the farm and then sent away at fourteen. The new home was graced by a momentous visit by my father, Joseph Victor in 1946. My father was now 77 years old and couldn't make the trip by himself. Mr. and Mrs. Joe Slopis of Beaumont, Texas drove him all the way to Maryland.

Visit from Joseph Victor – 1946
Left to Right: Doris, Richard, Jacqueline.
Seated: Joseph Victor

Richard and Granddad Hajek
(14 yrs old) (77 yrs old)

In 1949, I purchased the Moller mansion at 441 N. Potomac Street. It was the family home of the world-renown Moller Organ Company. First hand stories tell of how the elderly Mr. Moller would get up at 5:00 A.M. and crank-up the huge organ in his home waking everyone in the home and the neighbors. The

Moller Mansion, 441 North Potomac Street
The Maryland Medical Secretarial School - Hagerstown Business College

many rooms would offer classrooms dedicated to a specific type of class. It was much easier to set-up typewriters and adding machines for business/secretarial classes and medical charts for the medical secretarial curriculum in separate rooms. To house all of these new students in dorm-like accommodations, I contracted the Dagmar Hotel which was located downtown.

As an adjunct to the college, I formed The Maryland Medical Secretarial School. To house this new offering, I built another building behind the mansion. Things were going so well, that I purchased the Hoff Business School in Warren, Pennsylvania.

131

A year later I further expanded by obtaining the Jamestown Business School in Jamestown, NY.

Needless to say I was spreading myself pretty thin and the stress of juggling all these endeavors started to take its toll on my health. My weight increased, as did my blood pressure. Then I

started having what I called "little episodes" with my heart. The family doctor warned me to slow down and take better care of myself, but it was hard to slow down after seeing the fruits of all my years of hard work. I wanted to own my own school and now I had three.

My work ethic and lifestyle also affected my family. The hectic pace no longer permitted me to be a "hands-on" father. Dear Hettie basically raised our three children. In my generation the household revolved around the father. The father sat at the head of the table, was served first, children were quiet if father was reading or napping. One way I found to de-stress was reading True Detective magazines. I found myself getting lost in the stories and tried to solve the mystery before the detectives actually did. I read these magazines religiously. I would come home for dinner with the family and then go back to my office at the school and read them all evening. I'm ashamed to admit that I even read them in my office after I dropped the family off at Church and Sunday School. I didn't drink or smoke, so I called this my entitled addiction.

Chapter 20

Heir Apparent

1953

Many momentous events took place in 1953. Dick graduated from his beloved VPI, Virginia Polytechnic Institute in Blacksburg, Virginia (VA TECH). He was a son that any father would be proud of. He thrived in their military environment, despite the hazing during his "rat" (freshman) year. He rose to Cadet Major in the VPI Corps of Cadets and graduated with a BS in Business Administration. In addition, he was commissioned in the Air Force as a 2nd Lieutenant. Upon graduation, he was sent to school at the Lowery Air Force Base in Denver, Colorado. He told me about his short days of school and long nights of drinking with his buddies at the Bachelor Officers Quarters (BOQ) where they could get cheap drinks and a fancy room for $1 per night. Apparently drinking and chasing "skirts" was the Air Force creed. He and his buddies would go the local dance clubs, sure to pick up some girls.

Richard J. Hajek VPI (VA TECH) 1950

At the age of 23, he completed his training and was assigned to Westover Air Force Base in South Hadley Falls, Massachusetts, as an Intelligence Officer with the 337th Fighter Interceptor Squadron. He and his buddies would continue to spend their free time "chasing skirts", he sheepishly admitted to me when asked. One Saturday evening his buddies invited him along to a local dance. He was slightly reluctant since he didn't have a date. Razing like guys do, they assured him that his good looks would land him a girl in short order.

Having just been backed into a corner, he said "Sure, I'll go along and show you jerks just how it's done".

Saturday evening rolled around quickly and Dick straightened his tie in the mirror of his room at the Bachelor Officers Quarters. He looked dashing in his new suit, glad to be out of his uniform for the evening. He was ready for whatever the night would bring.

"So where are you guys taking me tonight? I hope it's a nice place where I can work my magic."

They laughingly said "we're off to a social at Smith College in North Hampton, Massachusetts; plenty of girls there, Romeo."

"Sounds good to me, bring them on. I feel lucky tonight."

And lucky he was! Shortly after they entered the social hall, he spotted a beautiful young lady with blonde hair and a face that would melt any guys' heart. He made his way across the room and introduced himself. They hit it off immediately with small talk.

"Would you like to dance?" he asked with that devilish grin of his.

She graciously accepted and took hold of his outstretched hand. They danced and talked, getting to know each other as the hours passed.

Dick said, "You seem different than the other girls that I've met here at South Hadley Falls or Springfield".

"That's because I'm from New York City. You know what they say about New York City girls!"

"Well, I've heard a lot about you girls, but which trait are you referring to?"

She said, "The one that declares that we are highly intelligent women and date guys of the same caliber only."

"Well, then today is your lucky day, for I am an Intelligence Officer in the Air Force!" They both had a good laugh and continued to dance as he twirled her in a circle.

Dick said, "So tell me about yourself, starting with your name."

He learned Ellen Spears actually came from a middle class family who sacrificed everything to send their daughter to a fancy college. Ellen told him she was determined to make them proud of her. Somehow the two of them just clicked and they danced the night away.

They dated exclusively for months, growing closer as time went on.

"Would you like to drive me to NYC for the weekend and meet my parents? You can stay in our guest room so it won't cost you much. My parents are dying to meet this terrific guy who has monopolized my time while at college."

"Sure, I'd be honored to meet your family. Besides, I've never been to the Big Apple and it sounds like a great weekend."

He picked up Ellen at Smith College Friday afternoon after they both completed their duties. It was a gorgeous drive down to the city and they relished every moment of their time together. They had a great time telling stories about their childhood and college antics. Dick was slightly apprehensive about driving into Manhattan, but Ellen assured him she was a good co-pilot, a necessity for an Air Force man. She guided him through the bustling streets and they parked right in front of her parents' apartment building. Mr. and Mrs. Spears met them at the front door and seemed equally happy to see Ellen and her new beau.

New York City was almost overwhelming to a guy from a small town in Maryland. They walked the streets taking in the sights and enjoying the local cuisine. Her parents splurged and bought them tickets to see a play on Broadway Saturday evening. The weekend went by much too fast and they found themselves heading back to Massachusetts late Sunday afternoon. They both were developing deeper feeling and secretly wondering whether this romance would lead to something more serious.

Dick was always a personal kid, keeping things close to his vest, not one to share details. Hettie and I were both shocked and thrilled when he called and told us he had been dating a girl exclusively for the past year. It didn't surprise us as he cut a striking pose in his Air Force uniform and that trademark, devilish smile. Dick always had a sharp mind, quick sense of humor and a kind heart, all endearing qualities in a man now starting to think about taking a wife.

Ellen graduated with honors from Smith College and her parents made another sacrifice by sending her to Europe for the summer. It was hard for them to say good-bye, but Ellen knew she would be back in Dick's arms in 10 weeks. Dick went on with his duties at the Air Force Base that was responsible for patrolling the DEW (Defense Early Warning) line on the Canadian border. The US government was sure the Russians would try to come over the border, prompting them to have several small radar bases stretching from East to West.

VPI 1ˢᵗ Battalion Staff
Richard Hajek, Cadet Major (Second in Command)
(Second from the Right)

Chapter 21

HANDING OVER
THE REINS

1954

Then suddenly in the fall of 1954, one of my little heart episodes landed me in the hospital. I had a full-blown heart attack. It was at that moment that I knew three things. I needed to sell those other two schools immediately. The logistics of managing schools that far away just didn't make it prudent any longer. The second thing I needed to do is talk Dick into leaving the Air

1st Lieutenant Richard J. Hajek, USAF

1st Lieutenant Richard J. Hajek with 2 Airmen

Force and come back home to run the college, with my help of course. I will be 65 in December and the doctor said I had to either quit or at the very least, go part-time.

I called Dick and talked to him about changing careers. It was a tough sell because he loved the Air Force. Currently he was a 1st Lieutenant, and planned to make a career of the military. He received his commission just as the Korean War was winding down and never had to go overseas, thank God.

His refusal stunned me, realizing that my power as the "head of household" reached only so far. Sensing my desperation, Hettie and the girls wrote letters pleading with Dick to come home to save Father and the college. Dick and his Mother were very close and he finally relented to constant pleading. He announced his decision to leave the Air Force to his drinking comrades and reluctantly came back to Hagerstown in 1955. Dick's life had already been turned upside down when Ellen wrote to him stating that she planned to stay in Europe. She stumbled upon a job and met a guy who stole her heart.

The first thing Dick did when he got home was buy himself a brand new 1955 Pontiac Grand Prix with the money he had been saving for an engagement ring no longer needed. He paid $3,500 for his stylish tan and bronze sporty-looking ride. Even though I was conservative having survived the Great Depression, I never said a word about his extravagant purchase. If it helped to heal his broken heart and find a little revenge for being dumped, so be it.

The third thing I had to do before I left this earth was get right with God. My Catholic religion, my years as a Priest all came flooding back to me. I realized how foolish I had been all these years defying God and my Mother. She passed away in 1943 without having laid eyes on her grandchildren. I only saw her twice in my adult years; once when I preached at her church in West in 1916 and second during my visit just before she died. How sad! I contacted the Priest in Williamsport, told him the whole story and confessed my sins. I began the required instructions to be reinstated as a practicing Catholic. Of course, I had to do all this without Hettie or Dick knowing the slightest detail. Doris and Jacqueline were both married and living their own busy lives by now.

Sometimes Gods ways are hard to understand. Leaving the Priesthood and teaching all these years enabled me to help thousands of students get their lives on track. In retrospect, God put me in the right place, doing the right work. Joseph was right all those years ago when he said we Hajeks were entrepreneurs. One must wonder how much of our lives we're allowed to choose or how much is decided before we are even born.

Dick coming back to Hagerstown was the best thing for the school and me. He would later tell you it was the worst decision he ever made. He was very intelligent and had a head for teaching and business. Together we formed the National Legal Secretarial School. In addition, we obtained accreditation for all facets of the college. We became the first proprietary school in the state of Maryland to receive degree granting status for the Associate Degree. In late 1956, Doris's husband, Dave Drawbaugh, joined the business as part owner, Treasurer, and math teacher. We all agreed that we had a strong team in place to insure the college's future. To accommodate the ever increasing student base, we purchased the Stickle Mansion next door to the school. We moved all administrative offices, conference rooms and the library to this building to free up more space for much needed classrooms.

Life was progressing normally for our family when I received a call that my Father was in the Waco Hospital in grave condition. My sister, Mary, had been caring for him in his home for several months. He was now 87 years old and God was calling him home. The family told me not to rush getting back to Texas as the doctors told them he would pass-on that very day. He died on March 3, 1956 with his grandson, Edward W. Hajek and his wife, Nina, at his bedside. I made the trip home for his funeral with the idea I would finally be able to be seen in public. My mother had long since passed-on to what I could only imagine as a "gold plated room in Heaven" for her life of faithfulness. Most of the citizens of West that remembered anything about me were probably deceased also.

My fathers' funeral was a large event since he was one of the founding fathers of West and lived there almost 40 years. He was well liked by everyone that ever met him. After the funeral, as per Czech custom, the men went to the local bar and drank beer until the women readied their favorite Czech dishes. As the women worked, they reminisced about how kind my Father was and how devoted he was to his late wife, Juliana. All the cousins remembered that he gave them dimes to buy candy at the local store and always gave them lots of Easter candy. The men sensing it was about time for the big meal, bought more beer and took it back to Dads' house on Davis Street. Czech men drinking beer was a long standing custom, so the beer and food flowed all day. It was a massive celebration of a life well lived.

On my way back to Hagerstown, I got that funny feeling all siblings get after they just buried their last parent; knowing that your generation is now on the firing line, the next to leave this earth. It also makes one take a hard look at his own family and appreciate what he has. I was grateful for a loving wife, two lovely daughters and a devoted son. Dick's broken heart eventually healed and he met another young lady. He planned to be married in 1957 and start his own family, thus fulfilling my dream of carrying on the family name.

It's now the early 1960's and I find myself sitting in my office at school starring out the window. My mind wondered back over the formative years of the college, the years of expansion and now the years of accreditation. Enrollment was up to 400 students. Dick had long since taken over some of the teaching, the never ending task of high school recruitment and the administrative side. I was proud that the college had a superb reputation in the community and that I achieved what I set out to do so many years ago.

Three Divisions of Hagerstown Business College

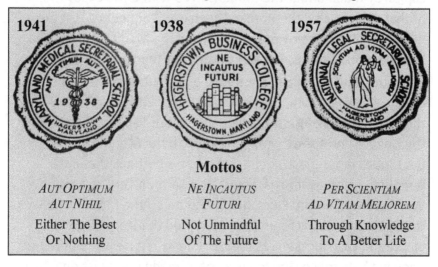

1941   1938   1957

Mottos

Aut Optimum	*Ne Incautus*	*Per Scientiam*
Aut Nihil	*Futuri*	*Ad Vitam Meliorem*
Either The Best	Not Unmindful	Through Knowledge
Or Nothing	Of The Future	To A Better Life

Things were going so well that I surprised Hettie with a long overdue vacation. She always wanted to visit the Holy Lands and a local travel agency was sponsoring a 10 day tour. Hettie was so thrilled to finally take her "trip of a lifetime" and for just the two of us to have some quality time.

"Oh Edward, it will be so wonderful to get out of Hagerstown with no students or parents calling the house, no building maintenance problems - - - just you and me."

"Here are the tickets and the itinerary, Dear. All you have to do is pack for us both." Hettie promptly called Doris and Jacque to share the good news.

I was making the supreme sacrifice for Hettie for I had mixed feelings about this particular trip. Half of me was anxious to see where Jesus walked and see the places come to life that I studied about in seminary. The other half of me wondered whether this trip would bring me back to God and the Catholic Church or just deepen the guilt that still raged in my heart. Only time would tell as we embarked on this adventure.

We took the train from Martinsburg, West Virginia to New York City to catch our flight to Tel Aviv. The next morning our tour guide took our group along the coastal plain to Caesarea, capital of Judea under the Romans. We visited the excavations of that ancient city, the Roman theatre and aqueduct. On our way to Galilee, we saw port cities along the Mediterranean Sea and the world famous Persian Gardens at the Bahai Temple.

In the days to follow, we took a boat cruise on the Sea of Galilee to Capernaum, the center of Jesus' Galilean ministry and the site of many of His miracles. We visited Tabgha, the site of the "loaves and fishes" story and then to the Mount of Beatitudes where Jesus delivered what *is* perhaps the most famous sermon ever preached --"The Sermon On The Mount". When we walked the Palm Sunday Route on the Mount of Olives to the Garden of Gethsemane and visited the Upper Room where the Last Supper was held, my heart felt heavy with regret. Knowing how much God loves all of us made me question why I ever weakened and broke my vow of Chasity. Surely I could have pulled myself back from the brink. But I also know from my years of living and learning life's lessons that God has a master plan. He sent Jesus to atone for our sins and I know without a doubt that I have been forgiven. After all, I was a 27 year old virgin who happened to fall in love with a beautiful young lady. How can that be a sin?

Taking this trip was probably another piece to God's master plan. I came to realize a deep sense of peace, prayer and self-forgiveness. I would continue my instruction on becoming a member in good standing of the Catholic Church when I got back home. Maybe someday I might even tell Hettie and my children of my years as a Priest - - maybe?

After a wonderful vacation and a safe flight back to New York City, we were eager to board the train back to Martinsburg. I was unusually tired but just chalked it up to the strenuous itinerary and the emotional tug-o-war I experienced with my faith and not being able to share any of my feelings with Hettie. We were passing through New Jersey when I felt ill and stood up to go to the men's room. I took two steps and passed out cold. The next thing I remembered was waking up in a New Jersey hospital with my ever-faithful Hettie at my side.

"Where are we, Hettie, and what happened to me?"

"I guess the trip was too much for you, Edward. The doctors couldn't find anything wrong. They just want to keep you under observation for a couple of days."

It was at that moment that I truly felt my own mortality. I was so grateful for my wife, my family and my legacy of the college.

We made arrangements for Doris' husband, Dave, to drive to New Jersey to pick us up and take us back to Hagerstown. Good ole Hagerstown - - **our true home**. Of all the places we have been, this truly felt like home.

I eventually got back into my regular routine after a much needed rest. My weekly visits with Father Dauch had become more of an enjoyment than instructional. We had become close friends who enjoyed our conversations about theology and life in general. I was feeling good about my life and what I had accomplished. Most of all, I was eager to see what the future would bring for my family and the college. However, little did I know that a fatal heart attack was lurking around the corner.

So, now we're back where we started. February 5, 1963, I just suffered a massive heart attack and I'm lying on the bathroom floor with my razor still in my hand.

As I said in the beginning, I had a large wake where family and friends were as equally shocked at my sudden passing as they were at the Catholic style ceremony. The Priest had a small private funeral for my family and that was that. Done, gone, my whole life a memory. Father Dauch never told the family that due to strict Canon Law, I could NOT have an ecclesiastical funeral mass in the church. It would have been completely unacceptable for a "fallen" Priest to be buried in the Catholic Church. By insisting on the graveside service, he spared them the humiliation and kept my secret as my confessing Priest.

Hettie would slowly adjust to living alone, Dick would continue to run the college, Doris, Jacque and their spouses would go back to their daily routines. To settle his curiosity, Dick visited Father Dauch in Williamsport to try to understand why his Father was reaffirming his Catholic faith after deliberately avoiding church and its principles. He told Father Dauch that he always found it interesting that his Father could quote almost any verse from the Bible and explain its' meaning, yet almost never set foot inside a church. He came away only with the realization that his Father was baptized a Catholic and wanted to get his affairs in order. Father Dauch told him that my reoccurring heart episodes must have sparked a sense of impending doom.

"Now, only time will tell if the truth ever surfaces or if my life's story goes with me to the grave".

Chapter 22

TEXAS DISCOVERY

1979

Richard at
Hagerstown
Business College
– 1972

The years passed and Dick continued to grow the college and be a presence in the community, just like his Father. Doris' husband, Dave was his right-hand man and kept the college finances in check.

However, in 1979, Dick and the family decided it was time to sell the college after 42 years in business. Technology was at the forefront and a major investment would have to be made to keep up with the never ending demands. National Resources out of Rockville, Maryland bought the school, buildings and accreditation rights. It was later sold to Kaplan University, a subsidiary of The Washington Post.

Dick went on to a successful career as a stockbroker and financial advisor. He loved working for "someone" else and not having to worry about enrollment and building maintenance. His people skills and teaching skills were the perfect match for explaining investment strategies. The widow ladies particularly loved him because they trusted him explicitly. His name was well known in town having taught over 10,000 students over a 28 year period he was at the school. They all had parents and probably children of their own by now, so his reputation preceded his new career. His success with the brokerage company earned him lavish vacations yearly as prizes for production. Dick remarried in 1988, enabling him and his new wife, Beverly, to live the good life.

Then in 1990 they decided to visit Texas to do some research on me, his Father. The nagging question still haunted Dick about his Fathers' religion. Something just didn't ring true and he wanted to find the truth if there was any truth to be found. They drove to Texas like typical tourists, visiting Fort Worth, a rodeo and then drove south on Route 35 toward the town of West. They turned off the highway into West, pulling off the road to get their bearings.

Dick said, "I wonder if we're in the right place?"

Bev looked up, spotting a street sign reading "Hajek Road". "Yes, I think we're in the right place, Dick."

They drove around the small town, population 2,485, seeing signs claiming to be the Czech Capital of Texas. Familiar businesses appeared such as Nemecek's Meat Market and the West Furniture Company. They went into the famous bakery to have their first taste of kolaches and talk to the locals. After introducing himself, the locals promptly told Dick he was pronouncing his name wrong. It was pronounced Hyak, not Hike.

Road in West, Texas
Named After
Joseph Victor

After hours of chatting, they left West more filled with kolaches than information about me. They continued south on Route 35 toward San Antonio. They did all the touristy things, including the River Walk, Alamo and wonderful meals and then decided to visit the Texas Institute of Culture. It was a marvelous two story building dedicated to preserving the different cultures of early immigrants who settled in Texas. They enjoyed the exhibits, took some pictures and bought a couple of books about the Czech heritage from the gift shop. Their next stop was Galveston, a coastal town known for its huge rock wall along the waters' edge and its humidity. The rock wall acted as a buffer from the frequent hurricanes. People actually put down their towels on top of it and laid in the sun. The humidity was unbearable causing water to run down the windows and faucets in their motel room to rust prematurely.

It was in that motel room that Dick made his first discovery about my past life. All those years of suppressing the truth was about to explode. Dick was propped-up on the bed reading one of the books purchased from the Texas Institute of Culture gift shop.

Suddenly he sat erect and yelled. "Bev, Oh My God, my Father was a Priest". It says so right here on page 263 of Krasna'

Amerika: A Study of the Texas Czechs, 1851-1939. Two guys named Clinton Machann and James W. Mendl wrote it. That's why he was renewing his faith towards the end of his life. He must have sensed that his heart issues were more serious than he let on to us".

A thousand questions raced through his mind all at once.

"Bev, why did he leave the Priesthood? How did he end up on the east coast while all his family stayed in Texas? Why didn't he ever tell us? I have to call Doris and Jacque immediately. They will be as stunned as I am."

"Good Grief, I wonder if your Mother knew that your Dad was a former Priest? Here are the phone numbers for your sisters."

Frantically he dialed the phone and delivered the revelation, the most shocking news to hit his family ever!

His sisters were flabbergasted initially, then they acted like big sisters do and said "Are you sure, Dick?"

"Yes I'm sure, I'm looking right at it. We're going to go back to San Antonio tomorrow and see what else we can find out. I'll let you know if I get any more details."

*   And just like that - - - a 75 year old secret was out of the bottle. They drove back to San Antonio and told the folks at the Institute about their finding. The staff was most gracious and offered to take them upstairs into their private library and research center. They gave them full access to their records, permitted them to make copies and take notes. Dick and Bev devoured the information and went away hours later, their heads swimming with facts and dates.

When they got back home to Hagerstown they showed the family what all they had uncovered but the search ended there for six more years. Bev's father died suddenly, plus she was about to make a major career change. After which, they both got caught up in their jobs and family, putting me on the back burner. It wasn't until 1996 that Dick decided to visit Texas again. Only this time he wanted to look-up his cousins who lived in Fort Worth and Burleson. It had been over 40 years since he saw his cousin, Edward, who was named after me. He was passing through Hagerstown many years ago while in the military and stopped by to see his Uncle Edward and Cousin, Dick.

The trip to Texas was all arranged and they were to meet the cousins at a local restaurant. When they walked in the door, the restaurant was packed with patrons.

Dick said, "How will we recognize Cousin Ed?"

Bev looked around the room and spotted Edward immediately.

Dick said, "How do you know that is him?"

Bev laughed and said, "Well just look at him, he looks just like you!" From that moment on Dick and Ed were glued together. They relished each-others company, laughed while swapping stories and jokes. It was nice Dick and Bev were finally getting to know the Texas cousins and form a lasting bond. Ed was a very successful businessman having built a large excavating business from the ground up. He also owned several ranches, a vineyard and partnered in several other small businesses. He was a kind soul with a larger-than-life personality. Everyone loved him.

During the next couple of days Ed gave them a tour his home, businesses and of West. By this time they had talked about me several times, each time peeling back the onion of my past. Ed was a fountain of information because his Father, Joseph, probably knew more about me than anyone on this earth. Guys will be guys and I'm sure Joseph told his son, Edward things that he would never tell his daughters.

During the tour they visited Nemecek's Meat Market where Joseph and I rode mules from the farm almost every day to pick-up meat and take it to the Priest and Nuns. Ed bought four pounds of smoked hot dogs, cold, right out of the meat case, insisting they all eat several while driving over to the cemetery. He had just treated everyone to a wonderful Czech lunch at one of the restaurants in West. He was such a loveable guy that no one wanted to hurt his feelings, so they stuffed themselves with Nemecek's hot dogs even though they were bursting from the big meal they just consumed.

West, Texas

The cemetery was an eye opener for them. It was well maintained with tombstones dating back to the 1800's. Ed told them that you had to be three things to get into this cemetery in West; Catholic, Czech and dead. They were fascinated by some of the tombstones that had pictures of the person inset in the marble stone. Some of the stones were so old that the names and dates were starting to diminish, yet the picture was clear as a bell. I remember my Father telling me that having a picture on a tombstone was a common custom in old Czechoslovakia. The Czechs were famous for their porcelain, so they drew the conclusion that the picture was protected by clear porcelain poured into the recess over top of the photograph.

It was during that cemetery visit that a major piece to their puzzle came to light. Ed took Bev aside, pretending to show her another interesting tombstone.

"Bev, I like you and trust you and I need to share some information with you after which you can decide whether or not you thought Dick would want to know".

Bev couldn't imagine what Ed was about to tell her, but she agreed to his terms. He proceeded to tell her everything he knew about my romance with Evelina, the strong possibility of a daughter and my leaving the Priesthood. **She was enthralled by his recollections and it was at that very moment that I knew I finally had my means of relaying my story. It was that very moment that she knew that someday she wanted to write a book about my life.**

That evening back at the motel, she and Dick went for a walk and she told him everything Ed confided in her at the cemetery.

Dick was shocked at first and then said, "I don't blame Dad for wanting a wife and a normal life. However, I'll never understand why he didn't tell his own family. When I think back now, I'm sure that even my Mother never knew. I suppose he had his reasons. It will take me some time to digest all this news and make sense of it. However, until we think this through, I think we should promise each other that *this* secret should stay between us. What purpose would it serve to tell the rest of the family? My dad's life was a mystery, so let's just leave it like that".

Bev said, "I understand, it's totally up to you."

They had plenty to talk about on the long drive back to Maryland. They felt good about finally having some answers regarding my past, but each answer just beckoned more questions.

Joseph V. Hajek
1867 - 1956

Juliana K. Hajek
1869 - 1943

Vilem Hajek
1893 - 1901

Juliana Hajek
1901 - 1902

Chapter 23

THE VESSEL

2015

The years passed and she would dream of writing her book, but life got in the way. Besides, it wouldn't be a good book unless Dick gave her permission to tell the whole story. For twenty years, she would make notes, write pages, and lay-out chapters. She even had the title and cover design in her head, but that's as far as it was going to go. Over the years, Dick would drop little tidbits of information for the family. Finally 15 years deep into their retirement in 2015, Dick said it was time to tell the world about his Dad.

He said "If you want to write a book, my father and I would be honored."

That's all she needed to hear. Months of research followed, conversations with family and one last trip to Texas was planned. There she talked to relatives, who were all well into their 80's by now. She was so grateful for their support and the knowledge they imparted. They visited towns and places that my Father and I frequented. Unfortunately, Cousin Ed died in

2005, taking with him invaluable information about me. She designed a family tree, created timelines on each generation, read books and articles, and found old photos.

Coincidently, on the 100th anniversary of my ordination, June 18, 1915, she began to write. She wasn't even aware of the significance of the date when she finally put thoughts to paper until she looked up a reference date. She actually got cold chills when she realized the correlation. As it turned out, writing was the easy part. Words flowed like water after being penned-up for twenty years. Days, weeks and months passed, pages filled one by one. It was such a relief to see my story come to fruition, correcting the wrong that I did by concealing my past.

Bit by bit, paragraph by paragraph my story started to come together. She had two cork boards in her office, one with old photos and one with the family tree and timelines. As she typed she wondered whether she had gotten into my head OR if I were in hers. Whichever it was, there definitely was some kind of connection. Somehow my story started to make sense to her and she actually felt like I was guiding her words. She would stop and stare at the old photos, taking time to analyze the facts and try to picture how things were back then. I could feel her looking directly into my eyes on the photo and then our thoughts clicked again. Her fingers began to fly over the keyboard and I could sense her excitement.

She told Dick one day, "Sometimes I look at your Dads picture and thoughts pop into my head. I honestly think your Dad is channeling his message through me."

She didn't take this writing lightly. She took a course on "Creative Non-fiction Writing", met with two published authors to learn more about writing techniques and how to get published. She talked with a former Priest who explained the burial process and how in 1915 there was NO MERCY for leaving the Priesthood. It was at that moment she understood why Father Dauch was trying to guide the family toward a simple graveside funeral service. She understood that Father Dauch was honoring my request of not telling my family about being a Priest and secondly, he knew that I could not have a funeral mass in the Catholic Church. In the Catholic religion I was considered a **Notorious Objector of the Faith** and not worthy to have a funeral mass in the church or to be buried on blessed ground or a Catholic cemetery. To do so, would have been scandalous. The sense of shame was a powerful tool used by the Catholic Church. Even after the Canon Law was updated in 1917, there was NO MERCY for wayward Priest. I guess the Catholic Church never bought into the saying "All Saints have a Past and All Sinners have a Future"!

Bev even contacted the Director of Archives & Records at the Archdiocese of Galveston-Houston, who gave invaluable information about me and my time at the seminary. Everyone she spoke to provided her with another piece to my puzzle. Until one day she declared it finished. She was finally comfortable with her research, the flow of the story and the facts presented.

I was pleased with her adaptation of my life and my soul. In fact, I even felt a little guilty for having "used" her as my vessel. Perhaps she was my last student and I her muse. In Webster's New World Dictionary a "muse" is defined as: The spirit regarded as inspiring a poet or other artist, source of genius or inspiration.

It took over a hundred years to right the wrong of my storm-vexed life and now I can finally "Rest in Peace" and my soul can leave this earth. I have made peace with God and received His everlasting forgiveness. **I had to wait 100 years before someone was willing to tell MY story, MY way.**

SOURCES

		By:
1.	"Krasna Amerika"	Machann, Mendl
2.	"The Hajek Family Tree"	Pauline Hajek Taylor
3.	"Czech Pioneers of the West"	E. Hudson & H. Maresh
4.	"Presenting The Catholic Faith"	Frank P. DeSiano, C.S.P.
5.	"We're Czechs"	Robert Skrabanek
6.	"A History of the Czech-Moravian Catholic Communities of Texas"	Rev. V. A. Svrcek
7.	"Texas Historian"	Volume XLV, Sept. 1984
8.	"A Chronology of Czech"	Settlements in Texas
9.	"Short Biographies of Czech & Other Priests in Texas"	Alois Morkovacy
10.	"The 1900 Storm".com	The Daily News
11.	"The History of Saint Mary's Seminary, La Porte, TX"	Father James F. Vanderholt
12.	Diocese of Galveston-Houston	Lisa May, Director of Archives
13.	"Battle on the Bay: The Civil War Struggle for Galveston"	Edward T. Cotham, Jr.
14.	"The Transmitter"	Vol. Eleven, October 1923

SITES VISITED:

1.	Texas Czech Heritage Center, Inc.	La Grange, TX
2.	Texas Institute of Culture	San Antonio, TX
3.	West Museum	West, TX
4.	West, Fort Worth, Burleson, La Grange, Fayetteville, Cat Springs, Galveston and Rosenberg, TX	
5.	Hagerstown Historical Society	Hagerstown, MD

ONLINE RESEARCH:

1. Wikipedia.org/various online sites
2. The Handbook of Texas – St. Mary's Seminary – Texas State Historical Society (TSHA)
3. The Role of Priests in the Catholic Church
4. Priesthood (Catholic Church)
5. History of Nashville, TN
6. Czech Names
7. The Handbook of Texas – Rosenberg
8. Handbook of Civil War – Texas
9. West, TX
10. Basilian Fathers, Congregation of St. Basil
11. Photos from World War One Photos archive www.WWIPhotos.com

INTERVIEWS WITH:

1.	Richard J. Hajek	Son of Edward J. Hajek
2.	Jacqueline H. Werner	Daughter of Edward J. Hajek
3.	Juliette Hajek Taylor	Niece of Edward J. Hajek
4.	Norma Lee Hajek Daniels	Niece of Edward J. Hajek
5.	Helen Hajek Brookes	Niece of Edward J. Hajek
6.	Sharon Hajek Matzner	Niece of Edward J. Hajek
7.	Edward W. Hajek	Nephew of Edward J. Hajek
8.	Nina Hajek	Wife of Edward W. Hajek
9.	Jeffrey Thoms	Former Priest

In Loving Memory
Of

Edward J. Hajek